Reflections

Australian Stories from My Father's Past

Helen Brown

Reading Stones Publishing

Copyright © Helen Brown 2020

ISBN Softcover   978-0-6488938-4-4
            eBook   978-0-6488938-5-1

All rights reserved. No part of this book may be reproduced or transmitted in any form or by any means, electronic, or mechanical, including photocopying, recording or by any information storage and retrieval system without the permission in writing by the copyright owner.

Unless otherwise stated Scriptures quoted here are from the King James Version (Authorised version). First published in 1611. Quoted from the KJV Classic Reference Bible, copyright 1983 by the Zondervan Corporation.

Any people depicted in stock imaginary provided by Shutterstock are models and are being used for illustration purposes only

Published by: Reading Stones Publishing
                             Helen Brown & Wendy Wood
                             woodwendy1982.wixsite.com/readingstones

Cover Design: Wendy Wood
Cover Photography: Lionel Morris

For more copies contact the publisher at:

Glenburnie Homestead
212 Glenburnie Road
ROB ROY NSW 2360
Mobile: 0422 577 663
Email: hbrown1956 1@gmail.com

Contents

Introduction

Boiling the Billy	1
Forgiveness	3
Oh, to be Valued	5
Water	6
Nature Trips	8
The Pit	9
The Broken Water Bag	11
Mr Armstrong	13
Hiding a Horse	14
Aeroplanes	16
A Memory	17
Moving a Stubborn Goat	19
Being a Christian at School	21
Hope	23
Swimming	25
Shelter in a storm	26
After to Storm	28
Gifted	30
Smart Dark Horse	32
Small Beginnings	34
Boys will be Boys	36
Two Lessons	38
Teaching a Young Dog	40
Advice to live by	42
Pink Sheets	44
Retraining	46
Family the Great Gift	48
Last Request	49
Learning from the Trees	51
Father's Call Home	53
Home on a Wing and a Prayer	55
Keeping Silent	57
A Missing Brother	59

Dreams	61
Modern Living	63
Alive and Kicking	65
Thief	67
Commitment	68
Under New Management	69
The Last Cup of Coffee	71
Guest Speaker	72
A Snake and a Cat	75
Buying a Shack	76
Fake or Real	78
God's Comfort	79
Stop, you don't need to go	81
Another Fake	83
Easter Inspirations	84
Deceived	86
Angels	88
Healing Hearts	90
New Year and Eternity	92
Puppets	94
New Life	96
Power of Prayer	98
Saved	99
The Spark	100
A Good Servant	101
Faithful to the End	102
Bush Skills	103
Salvation for a Gambler	105
Sweating it Out	106
Grandma's Wine	107
Someone Cares	109
Built on Rock Foundations	110
Healing with the Help of a Goat	112
Homemade Remedies and Prayer	113
Signs to Follow	114
A Destroyed Piano	115

Penicillin	116
What Happened to...	118
Bundaberg Anzac Padre Hero	120
Leather Shoes	123
My Town	125
Christmas changes the World	128
Pioneers	130
The Cross of Peace	132
Mission Settlements	133
Fishing at Sea	135
No Boomerangs	136
Sunday Lunch in the Outback	137
Scurvy	138
Under Steam Power	139
Sails to Steam	141
A Bird's Profanity	142
The Headstone	143
Life Saving Water	144
Equality	145
Taught by Experience	146
Bogged	147
Pulling Scrub	149
Fire	151
God Giveth	152
Making Hay	154
Bulls	156
In A Bar	158
Caring	159
What a Friend	160
Discipline	161
Found Out and Seeing Clearly	163
Three Blind Mice (or Dead Mice)	164
Outback Chaplaincy	165
Meeting People	166
Peace	168
Mozzies come to Church	169

Is this Texas	171
Sleeping Rough	172
Getting on the Sauce	173
A Drunk Preacher	174
A Drunken Preacher Sober	175
A Wise Woman	177
Texas	178
The Mysteries of God's Working	179
The Silent Passenger	181
Prisoner	183
Sleeping in Peace	184
A Visitor	186
A Working Holiday	188
A Night-time Visitor	190
Floods	192
Upgraded	194
Returned Thanks	196
Flooded	197
The Last Swagman	199
Christmas Prayers	201
Those Good Old Days	203
Preachers' Mistakes	205
A Nesting Hen	207
Off to Darwin	209
Still off to Darwin	211
The effects of War	213
Leprosy	215
Saying Grace	217

Introduction

We cannot change the past, yet it is the past that will teach and shape us and our future generations into who we, and they, are. No matter who we are, we are all sinners in the eyes of God until He steps into our history. It is how we respond to that intervention that will not only help shape our futures but also the generations that follow us.

It is because of the response of my great grandfather, grandfather, and father, that I have been able to learn much of what I share in books that I write. "Reflections – Australian Stories from my Father's Past" will explore many of the events that shaped the men in my life, who were faithful to God, and passed on those lessons to our generations.

Let me introduce my family to you:
Samuel Morris (born Southampton, England, 13 January 1856) – became a Christian in 1888 before his marriage to Emily Piggot (21 March 1894).
He was a blacksmith by trade and worked in various locations until he arrived in Inverell, New South Wales, Australia.
Their children were: Eva, Alice, Eliza, Grace, Elsie, Wilfred, and Doris.

Wilfred (born Inverell 14 April 1904) married Elvie Gray (16 April 1930). Wilfred's parents paid his apprenticeship as a bootmaker and he carried on his own business in Otho Street, Inverell, until he went dairy farming at Dunreath on the Swanbrook Road just before World War II.
Their children were: Norman, Hilton, Rose, and Joy.

Norman (born Inverell 19 February 1931 married Jean Olwyn Deans (7 January 1956).

Their children were: Jean Helen (Brown), Alan, Lionel, Olwyn (Harris), and Ian.

Norman worked as a station hand as well as developing his own milk run business until he went into training as a Salvation Army Officer in 1953.

For over 100 years the Lord Jesus Christ has blessed our family, not only in and around the town of Inverell, but across many parts of Australia. God has shown His faithfulness to us, and many of the family have served Him through several forms of ministry. It is this background of service, travel, trials, and encouragement that inspired the articles my father wrote, which were first published in a newspaper, and which I have now been able to put together in this book. As I read these stories, I am very much aware of just how blessed I am to have a God who mapped out my life before it began.

As I share his stories and my reflections with you, may the God who has been faithful to us, remind you of just how much He loves you and, as you respond with gratitude and service, may you see more blessings as they rain down on you.

Author's Note: As some of these stories relate to times long past, some of them use the term miles instead of kilometres. For reference, 1 mile = approximately 1.6 Km.

Boiling the Billy

Modern version of a billy. Photo courtesy of Evie Brown

When we were growing up during the thirties, we had wood fires and heaters. Today, most people have all electric homes. There were wood heaters in the school which I attended, and boys were chosen daily to do fire duty. This meant that they had to start the fires and keep them burning throughout the day in the cold weather. In one of our homes, we had a wood heater doing its job when city visitors arrived.

The father stood by the heater and said, "It is wonderful to get warmth this way", and was anxious to show his boys how it worked. I was surprised to realize that the owners of modern homes knew so little about how we cooked and heated our homes in days gone by.

If we, as children, went to work with men on the farms, we had to boil the 'billy' for 'smoko'. We were taught where and how to set the fire so that it would not get out of control and to check the fire before we left, to see that it was safe. Men put their smokes out before they dropped them, or put them into their tobacco tins.

As a young boy, I remember being allowed to go camping with a cousin, travelling in a horse and cart. We went two kilometres from home to a well, got our water from a cattle trough, and lit the fire to boil the 'billy'. We slept under the cart at night.

During the day, we hunted rabbits. We did not put our arms up hollow logs in case we found snakes instead of rabbits. Instead, we used number eight wire with mud on the end which stuck to the rabbit's fur and when we turned it over like a crank handle, it twisted and stuck to more fur and we were able to pull the rabbit out far enough to see. We could then pull it the remainder of the way by hand. These were some of the skills we learned from our elders.

It is important for young people to learn by the example and words of their elders how to live safely, healthily; emotionally, mentally, and spiritually. This way they learn the benefits and dangers of life and are set up to find fulfillment.

God gave these principles in Deuteronomy 5 and in Chapter 6:7, He said, "You shall teach them diligently to your children, and shall talk of them when you sit in your house, when you walk by the way, when you lie down, and when you rise up."

Reflection: Lord, I thank you for the good example the elders in my life have been.

Forgiveness

It was a time when very few people had motor cars and stores had horse yards for those who drove a horse and buggy. If you lived within a few kilometres of your destination, you walked. Mothers with young children had prams made of cane with room to carry their purchases as well.

Tradesmen made deliveries; the Milkman, the Baker, the Butcher, the Grocer, all with a horse and cart coming to your door. If you were away, the goods were left in a safe place. People were trusted not to steal your goods.

It was because of this, I learned about guilt. I came home from school one day to find that my Mother was not back from her shopping trip and the grocery delivery had been made. I was looking for an after-school snack and I had a choice, something I knew that I was allowed to have or something else. In those days, butter and sugar mixed together made a boy's Butter-scotch which I made right there on the verandah. The taste was so good but I also knew I had broken the trust that my parents had in me and I could not cover my wrong. There was going to be a consequence that I was not looking forward to. I had to escape. The house was high enough for a boy to get under, but too low for Mum, so under there I went. Of course, it was not long before I heard my mother calling "Where are you Norm?" Eventually in a guilty, shaking voice I made my whereabouts

Family Home in Auburn Vale Road Inverell

known. Disobedience, theft, guilt, and hiding had spoiled our relationship. Out I came to learn about reprimand, yet best of all, forgiveness from a loving Mother

When we become aware of our need of forgiveness, God has said: "If we confess our sins, He is faithful and just to forgive us our sins, and to cleanse us from all unrighteousness". 1 John 1:9.

Reflection: Dear Lord, I thank you that you care for us; not only for the way you teach us about our sins but also for your wonderful grace that forgives us when we repent.

Oh, to be Valued

As a boy, shopping with Mother in the old Department Store had its challenges. The counter was high and I had a job to look over it. The Grocer wore a white apron, and smiled. He weighed the sugar, biscuits, and other orders and you saw what you got. These days I have to put on my glasses to read the packages' small print for the volume, because the container can look big but sometimes the contents only take up half of the container.

When the Grocer tied the parcels with string, I was intrigued and watched how he flicked it around his finger and snapped it with a jerk. It was years before I learnt to do that!

Why are these lasting memories? They were special because people treated people as being important, including children.

Today the load speaker raucously tells us the "the meat or some other item is 'special', and people move around with a searching look on their faces. People need people whose actions are meaningful – Oh, to be valued!

When Jesus Christ explained how God values all things, He said in Luke Chapter 12:6-7; "What is the price of five sparrows? A couple of pennies? Not much more than that. Yet God does not forget a single one of them. And he knows the number of hairs on your head! Never fear, you are far more valuable to Him than a whole flock of sparrows."

Reflection: Oh Lord, I thank you that you value me more than the sparrows. Remind me to be thankful for this every day. Help me not to let myself, or others, devalue my life by putting me down.

Water

Being the oldest in the family, I can remember my parents putting their home together. This was before financial institutions said "have what you want now and pay later on." I think that the people who get caught up in these schemes can become slaves for most, if not all of their lives. To me it makes the Pharaohs or the tax collectors back in the biblical days look tame!

A water tank

My parents saved on everything, including water. We had 2 x 4,000 litre tanks, (about 2,000 gallons all up) so we washed in a dish on a stump near the garden, then the water went on the plants. Bathing was done once or twice a week in a round tub in the kitchen, in winter in front of the fire. The cleanest person went in first and the dirtiest last. Clothes were boiled in a copper. This was a large round tub made of copper with a fire underneath it to heat the water. It was usually housed in a shed in the backyard. After the washing was finished, the hot water was used to scrub the veranda and the Little House (the original environmentally friendly toilet) located up the back yard away from the house. How white the boards looked after that treatment! These days I enjoy the convenience of pressure water - hot and cold, and not going to the toilet up the yard. But saving that wonderful, life-giving and cleansing gift of water is still important, because of my childhood experiences.

Jesus Christ used water as a means to explain how your inner personality can be given life everlasting. "But whosoever drinketh of the water that I shall give him shall never thirst; but the water that I shall give him shall be in him a well of water springing up into everlasting life" John 4:14.

Reflection: Father, I thank you that you have given to all those who believe in you, the gift of your Spirit which works in us daily, filling us with your presence, love, courage, and strength.

Nature Trips

Growing up in a country town when horse flesh was the means of transport, holidays between Christmas and New Year were spent visiting friends and relatives in a horse and sulky. When I see TV programs featuring bush walks, showing different vegetation and wild life, I realize that we didn't need that. For us it was a way of life.

The sulky was a 'three-seater'. We kids sat on the floor, hats were a 'must', and something to cover your knees was needed. At a few kilometres hour, we were told about and could see, as we travelled, the kinds of trees and their uses, bee's nests, bird's nests, and all the other variety of wildlife that abounded in the bush in those days. We identified the male and female birds by their colouring. We saw the different kinds of soil and the possible minerals to be found. We saw blue bells by the road, flowering trees with the pollen and learnt about the types of honey that they could give. We observed animals and their condition, if poor, we might have commented that they needed more care, or if in good condition, praising an efficient farmer.

Like any young boy, I must have talked too much, because when we saw sheep, my father would say "every time a sheep bleats, it loses a mouthful". Years have taught me that less talk and more action is what counts. Proverbs 10:19-21. "In the multitude of words there wanteth not sin: but he that refraineth his lips is wise.... The lips of the righteous feed many: but fools die for want of wisdom."

Reflection: Lord, please help me to listen to others, not only with my ears but with a prayerful heart and soul.

The Pit

Drought is part of our wonderful country. For boys in our district, our slippery dip was the gully banks when they were dry. Before this, there would be washed-out holes that would hold water after the gully had stopped running. They had a two or three foot perpendicular drop and as the dry worsened, the holes would finally become pits with sticky, muddy slush in the bottom.

On an afternoon's exploring walk along the Black Gully, a mate and I came to one of these holes about forty meters long and three meters across. My mate pushed me in and I was very quickly shin deep in the mud. The perpendicular banks meant that I could not get out. My mate got such a fright that he bolted for home leaving me struggling and bellowing at the top of my voice. The more I struggled, of course, the more I sank. I can't remember how long I struggled alone, but eventually my father came looking for me. When he came within earshot of my yelling, he was soon on the bank and hauled a dirty, frightened boy out. God bless caring fathers!

It reminded me of a comparison about a pit, *author unknown*.

THE PIT

Self-righteous – Only bad people fall into a pit.
Mathematician – Calculate the pressure that keeps you in the pit.
News Reporter – Wants rights of the story.
Fundamentalist – Deserve to be in the pit.
Realist – That's a pit.
Scientist – Calculate scientific reasons for the pit.
Geologist – Appreciate rocks – pit construction.
Evolutionist – You will die – we can't produce people that will fall into a pit
Shire Inspector – Did you get a permit to dig the pit?
Professor – Reasons for falling into the pit.
Self-pity – Have you seen my pit?

Optimist – Could be worse.
Pessimist – Don't worry – it will get worse.
Jesus - reached down and lifted the man out of the pit.

Reflection: Jesus, I want to thank you for coming down to earth. Thank for not only showing us how to live but for dying on the cross so that we can have our sins forgiven and be lifted out of our pits of sin.

The Broken Water Bag

My Dad was a boot-maker. In those days people often had only one pair of shoes. There were chairs for them to sit on while they waited for their shoes to be mended. Quite a few of the old men would just come in and talk, with many a remarkable story of early Australia being shared.

Waterbag & Saddle - Photo courtesy of Kilkivan Museum Queensland

One such story concerned a water bag. The water bag was rectangular in shape, made of quality canvas, a crockery spout coming out of the top corner and it had a wire carry handle which could be strapped to a horse drawn vehicle, to frames on running boards of early cars or the saddle of riding horses.

Two boundary riders were camped for the night out in western New South Wales. They broke camp early to head off in different directions. One rider rode off and as the second rider went to mount his horse, it swung around, dislodging his water bag, treading on it, and busting it. No water was left. The rider knew he was in big trouble. The nearest water was the Darling River, a day's ride away. He set off with care so as to conserve the energy of both horse and rider. As the sun rose and the day wore on, the sun beat down. He got a small stone to suck on in order to keep his mouth moist. After midday any shade looked inviting, but he knew that if he stopped, he would collapse and die, like others he had known to suffer their final fate in this way. Western heat is dry and unforgiving. It was a case of -'stay in the saddle – and keep the horse walking'. He knew he should meet the Darling River sometime in the late afternoon and at last – there it was with wonderful water! He lost control and rushed out waist deep and drank and drank which of course would mean certain death to a parched man.

The next thing he knew, two men grabbed his arms and told him he'd had enough. "Come on out, mate" they instructed, and thus rescued him from a watery grave. How great is our God! Of all the places he could have reached the Darling, he reached it at a spot where those two men were fencing – there was no one else around for miles.

His path was guided by God, fulfilling the promise of Proverbs 3:6: "He (God) shall direct thy paths".

Reflection: What a wonderful God you are oh Lord that you should direct us all in the way that you want us to go. Father, help us to listen for your directions when we read your word.

Mr Armstrong

I am a teetotaller, a decision I made partly because of advice from people who were not. The first I remember was from a man who, in my young mind, stood out. I will call him Sidney Armstrong. He was a big, well-built man. He was the first person I had met with a glass eye. He was the Caretaker of what us kids called 'the haunted house', which still stands on the Glen Innes Road. He was also an alcoholic. I know I was very young because I was sitting on the footstool which Dad used for customers, when he was fitting shoes in his Boot Shop.

On this particular day, in came Mr. Armstrong. "Sidney, you've been a naughty boy again", said Dad. "How do you know?" he replied. "Because you have forgotten your glass eye" was my father's response.

He bent down and looked into my face and in a concerned voice, said "Son, never have your first beer and you'll never be like me". (Mr. Armstrong, I have taken your advice!) What trouble, tensions and trials had he suffered to prompt him to try to protect this innocent, snowy-headed kid, we will never know. Even in this naughty state, as my father called it, he was willing to share a wisdom that he knew to be true.

The Bible tells us in Proverbs 4:10-11 "Hear, O my son, and receive my sayings; and the years of thy life shall be many. I have taught thee in the way of wisdom; I have led thee in the right paths".

Reflection: May I also have the humility to listen to those that you send into my life. As they share their stories, help me to learn more about how you would have me live oh Lord.

Hiding a Horse

Whitewash! I wonder how many know that it was used on lots of buildings in the early days of our country. Places such as the outhouses, dairies, and cream rooms were painted with this 'easy to apply' substance, using a brush that was broad with coarse bristles.

My mother told of a happening at their home farm. A man with the title of "The Cream Tester" came to test each cow. The idea was to see which cow gave the most cream. He was a Graduate from some Place of Learning. He came with his gear and travelled, as all people did in those days, in a Horse and Sulky. He had very little country experience. Testers did the afternoon milking, stayed at the farm overnight, with good old country hospitality, ready for the morning milking, and then they would travel to the next farm. Of course, the farmers were responsible for the care of the man's horse.

This new chum arrived in the new Government supplied "Turnout". Mum's two brothers met him, sent him in for a cup of tea and assured him that they'd care for his horse and gear. They promptly took the horse out of sight and gave him a full make-over of whitewash. Finally, they let him go with the other horses for his feed.

When the milk testing was over, it was time for the 'man of learning' to move on to the next farm. The boys were busy away with the herd, so this particular man had to find his own horse. He had come with a chestnut coloured horse and no matter how hard he looked: it appeared that it was not there. It took a long time, with much checking of the farm horses before the right horse was found, making him very late for the milking at the next farm and he was furious.

Boys will be boys! Thank God they will be men one day. The tester learned that he needed to know the quality and style of the horse, not just the colour, in order to be able to recognise which horse he was using.

God said in 1 Samuel 16:7 "....the Lord seeth not as man seeth; for man looketh on the outward appearance, but the Lord looketh on the heart". (I am glad about that).

Reflection: As my heavenly Father, I am so glad that you can see the motivation of my heart. Lord you know exactly what my intentions are, even when things come out wrong.

Aeroplanes

AEROPLANES! The first one I remember seeing was when my father took me to see the first landing of a plane in our district, on a flat piece of ground a little out of town. I was so small he barred me on his bike. That means I sat on the bar between the seat and the handlebars while he rode the bike from the seat. It was very hard on the bottom but easier than walking and better than not going at all. I remember the dust and the crowd of people looking in wonder at this flying machine.

On another occasion, not long afterwards, as I was walking across a paddock, there was a roaring noise not very high up in the sky. It was a two-engine plane. Looking back, I think it was an early Dragon Moth model. I was so scared, and as there was a horse trough about a half meter off the ground, I crawled under it, looking out with a very fast heartbeat, until the plane had passed over. I had never heard or seen such a contraption of that size. These were the beginnings of the air travel as we know them today, taking people around the world. We are even able to travel faster than sound.

What seemed impossible to my mind then, is now a reality. In the spiritual world the mind cannot take in all its possibilities but they are real. In 1 Corinthians 2:9-10 we read: "Eye hath not seen, nor ear heard, neither have entered into the heart of man, the things which God hath prepared for them that love Him. But God hath revealed them unto us by His Spirit: for the Spirit searcheth all things, yea, the deep things of God".

Reflection: We cannot know nor understand the scope of your imagination Lord, but I thank you that you are bigger than all my problems and you already have the answers prepared. Help me to walk in faith until you are ready to implement them.

A Memory

One day my youngest sister rang from New South Wales to see how her oldest brother was doing. I had sent her a birthday card and in it had written about a memory I had of her when she was just walking at about fifteen months of age.

Those were the days when we were using things which are now in museums. One piece of equipment was a Tree Jack. You dug around the tree, cut the surface roots, cut the Jack Spear high up into the trunk and then with a large five foot handle the Jack was ratcheted up to snap the tap root or else lay the tree over until you could cut the tap root. The spears, which were of different lengths, were made of H steel and very heavy.

I was eleven years old and sent to do my job of mixing the chook feed because there were no feed barns in those days. Someone had left a spear against the shed door to keep it open. My baby sister came to see what her brother was doing, when the wind blew the door and down came the spear. Only God knows how it only hit her little toe.

There were loud screams and lots of blood. I was in shock but grabbed her and carrying her, ran to mother at the house. I remember almost falling in my haste. I wanted it to be all right and tried to convince my mother so. She knew best and off she went to the Doctor with my baby sister in the pram. How long it took, who knows but it was no 'walk in the park'.

When they came home the toe was amputated. This taught me never to let my wishes affect my judgment.

When our spirits feel helpless, we can look in the Bible, and find many of God promises, one of which is; "Even I will carry, and will deliver you". Isaiah 46:4.

Reflection: Lord, I thank you for being able to carry us during those tough times in life. We may not feel as if we are being lifted but when we look back, we can see your great hand in our lives.

Moving a Stubborn Goat

Today's media often tells us about the short comings of our hospitals. When I was a child, local committees controlled the hospitals, with lots of voluntary contributions, the town considered it as "their own hospital".

Heating, hot water, and steam used for cooking and laundry etc came from a large boiler with a six foot or nearly two-metre-long fire box. To supplement the wood supplied by the contractors, and reduce the cost, the town authorities organized an annual wood parade to the hospital where the loads were stacked. The parade vehicles included early model motor lorries, horse drawn lorries, carts, drays, wagons and even boys with billy carts, all well loaded with wood. The vehicles lined up in the main street, paraded through the town, where a festival-like day was enjoyed by all.

Wood parade in the 1920's – Photo contributed to the Inverell Times for publication

My father watched from his boot makers shop, as the parade began, and saw a lad with a well loaded billy cart being pulled by a goat. The goat, however, refused to move when the others started. The boy pulled and poked. He could see his good deed and hard work being a failure and he was distressed. Several men tried to help, but the goat was going nowhere. A well-dressed man came to help, talked for a while, and walked away. My Dad thought this was an odd thing to do. After some minutes he returned with cabbage leaves which he attached to a long stick, tying one end to the wood in the cart and bringing the leaves over the goat's head out in front and just out of the goat's reach. As the goat moved to get the leaves, he pulled the cart and off they went, the leaves still out of reach, until they arrived at the hospital.

This showed that in our Country's early days we needed to work together to supply our needs and services.

In the Spiritual world, the Bible tells us in Colossians 4:19; "My God shall supply all your needs according to His riches in glory in Christ Jesus".

Reflection: Father, I thank you for supplying all my needs, you have given me much more than I could or would have asked for.

Being a Christian at School

Cooloola Christian College

The first school I attended, no doubt, had very committed teachers, but teaching methods were different to those used now. The cane was the accepted form of punishment, which meant that: each spelling mistake was worth one cut with the cane, moving after the bell had rung was worth another one. For bad misdemeanours you received six cuts.

For myself, in a school of several hundred students, to be identified as a believing Christian, was to be taunted with "Saved from sin, going to Heaven in a kerosene tin". Today, it would be called 'bullying'. In those days you either stood for Jesus Christ or you buckled. How schools have changed and what blessings and opportunities young people have today.

One November, I was privileged, as a Grandparent of one of the students, to attend the Cooloola Christian College Secondary Presentation night. The academic achievement was impressive. Sports awards were varied. The most important contributions to our country were recognised by the Citizen and Christian Character awards, which gave recognition for positive living, honest leadership, and moral behaviour.

At the same time, our State law-makers are increasing fines for law-breakers, which we hope will help but is unlikely to in the long run. The best remedy for reducing the number of lawbreakers is to put

Christian principles, such as this Christian College teaches, into action which is achieved by Godly living.

Proverbs 2:6 reads "For the Lord gives wisdom, from His mouth comes knowledge and understanding"

Reflection: Heavenly Father I thank you that our ancestors loved you and put into place many good laws to help our country be the place of safety that it is today. I also pray for all those who are trying to teach the younger generation, that they will remember that in order for this world to be a better place we must first be better people and that you are willing to help us do this.

Hope

Hope and Day Dreaming – what is the difference?

When I was a boy, Council work was done by horse power. Beautiful Clydesdale horses pulled graders, scrapers, ploughs, and drays.

My dream was to one day work for the Council, own the Clydesdale horses and have a small farm. To make that happen, it needed to become a hope which would put motivation into the dream. The wage then was about four pounds or $8 per week, if you had a job. How could such a dream happen? I saved every penny I earned or was given.

When the Education Department first sent Career Guidance Officers, and it was my turn to be interviewed, I was asked, "What do you want to be, what is your first choice?"
I answered, "A farmer"
What is your second choice?
"A farmer"
And your third choice?
"A farmer."
In an exasperated tone of voice, the advisor said "Go back to your class."

As things turned out, I did not use Clydesdale horses for power, work for the Council or own a little farm when I thought I would. There did however come a day when I did own more than one farm, used tractors for power and paid rates to the Council.

Day dreaming would not have achieved it, but hope, motivated work, and saving, turned what seemed an impossibility to the Guidance Officer into a reality. We all need hope, motivated work, and saving to make success ours.

In the Bible, Romans 8:24 reads "For we are saved by hope"

Reflection: I thank you Lord that you have a plan for my life. I thank you that you direct my paths. I pray that I will not be an idle day dreamer but an effective agent for you.

Swimming

When we were growing up, for the kids in our town, there were only rivers, creeks, dams, and one-piece swimming togs for swimming. This brought risks, especially if parents were distracted or the children too adventurous and could lead to drowning. My mother lost a younger brother in a river drowning. This made my parents very firm about staying away from water holes unless a responsible adult was present.

During summer months after school, mother took my brother and myself to the river to teach us to swim. After the lesson we enjoyed some special after school snacks. The river was quite wide, and when I had reached my tenth birthday, Dad joined us after work. I had to swim across the river and back again. I am not a keen water person, but I have never lost what I was taught about swimming.

Proverbs 22:6 says "Train up a child in the way he should go, and when he is old, he will not depart from it".

Reflection: Thank you Father, for the training that has been handed down to me through my parents.

Swimming at Inverell. Photo courtesy of Ruth Morris (nee Parsons)

Shelter in a Storm

When I was a child, house cows were the means by which many families got their daily milk supply. The cows were milked in the mornings, put out of the gates and they found their way to water at the creek or river. There they grazed for the rest of the day on the flats, known as the 'town common'.

The children's 'after school job' was to bring them in for the night. These animals became very quiet, being taught to lead and to be tethered up while being milked. There was no motor stock transport or horse floats in those days, so all animals were led or driven from place to place.

Few people in our circle owned cars. You walked, rode a bike - which only had twenty-eight-inch wheels in those days, and people often took another person on the bar between the seat and the handle bars, or you used horses, either ridden or towing a cart.

Our house cow was to be taken to my Uncle's farm ten miles away for a few months. To get her there, she would have to walk, so father decided to lead her with one hand and lead the bike with the other. In those days, he worked forty-four hours per week, which meant that on Saturday, he did not leave work until 1 pm.

There was at least a three hour walk to Uncle's farm. To make sure the cow travelled well, my seven-year-old brother and I (then ten years) were to walk behind the cow and keep her moving. The plan was for me to lead my bike out, and ride it back home while Dad barred my brother on his bike. It being summer time, with long daylight hours we should have been home before dark.

Things went well for the first four miles. Then in came what we called a "gully-raker" of a storm. We tethered the cow to a post and sheltered under a bridge. Down came logs and debris and the water broke its banks, so we backed up further under the bridge to escape the rushing water. I saw someone's canoe being swept by and my boyish mind thought "What a terrible waste". The storm lasted about an hour. By then it was too late for us boys to continue the journey, as it would be dark by the time we were to return. Dad sent us back home. We were struggling along the wet gravel road, one bike and two boys and had gone about half a mile when along came a man in a 1927 Dodge car.

He pulled up and gave us a ride. He put the bike between the mudguard and the engine and down on to the running board. He roped it on and two very tired boys had the ride of their lives in a car. He put us off in town and we walked the mile home, getting there in time for tea and bed. I have no idea what time Dad got home, but he was there for breakfast.

Here are the words of an old Hymn:
Home is home, however lowly, Home is sweet when love is there
Home is home, when hearts are holy, Earth has ne'er a spot so fair.
Jesus makes our home a heaven, sacred in the fireside warm.
After battling thro' the long day, Home's a shelter from the storm.

Reflection: Oh Lord, I thank you that as we go through the storms of life you are there to supply us with the necessary strength and peace to keep going.

[1] Arthur S Arnott – The Song Book of The Salvation Army 1970

After the Storm

Inverell Town Sign

I grew up in a town on the western slopes of the Great Dividing Range. The soil was very fertile; the climate was diverse and could be very cold and extremely hot. The town is surrounded by hills, some of them quite steep. The only way out of the town, without going uphill, was to follow the river which flowed North West.

The unusual geological formation of the area seemed to intensify the summer storms. I guess that they were not all that frequent, but I still remember several of them during my childhood.

One such storm came in just as I was bringing the house cow home. There was vivid lightning, cracks of thunder and driving rain. The cow refused to go forward and turned her back to the wind. I was forced to leave her and struggle back home, needing to come back to find her later.

At home, the bird cage had blown over, with some of the Canaries out and distressed. My first job was to gather them up and restore them to a cage before the cats made a meal of them. The eight-week-old chickens were scattered in all directions, wet, cold, and some stiff and almost buried in the mud. I had to collect them and account for the right number, and then Mother took over. The wood stove was burning, with the big oven door open, warming the room, where Mother put the cold and wet chickens into a box to regain their ability to chirp.

The ones which were stiff and appeared to be dead were wrapped in layers of towelling and put into the oven. The towelling absorbed the water and protected them from direct heat. The warmth brought life back, while I watched and waited. Within a short time, their legs moved, heads were raised and slowly they came to full movement.

To my young mind, it was a wonder. Where there appeared to be no life, there it was, restored before my eyes.

After the storm came the task of picking up the scattered objects around the yard and restoring order. With the benefit of hindsight, that storm taught me to deal with the important things straight away, for if left there will not be another opportunity.

This happened to the disciples of Jesus when they heard Him praying. They said "Teach us to pray". We now have the greatest prayer! Known to us as The Lord's Prayer in Luke 11:1-4.

Reflection: Lord help me to remember that I don't know what is around the corner of life, remind me to keep my candle trimmed and my light burning for you, so that when the end of my life comes, I will have very few regrets.

Gifted

As a boy growing up, one of the personalities I remember was a well-built man who lived about four kilometres out of town. He possessed a car, but quite often would walk to town. He kept the car mainly to take his wife shopping. On his few acres he kept a cow, poultry, and had a garden, but they had to be very water wise.

One year they grew lettuce for sale when there were practically none available. What he did was take a bucket of water every day and put a cup full at the roots of each lettuce. In this way, he produced an outstanding crop. This simple life-style gave them a fulfilling and enjoyable retirement. During his life, he had worked as an engineer in mining, keeping the steam engines running.

Among other things, he was also a gifted musician especially with brass wind instruments. He had played in a number of bands and been the Bandmaster of some. In those days, country concerts and suppers were a common way for people to enjoy themselves while raising funds for worthy causes. This elderly gent would play the trumpet with one hand and accompany himself on the piano with the other.

I had enough cheek to ask him where he had learned the piano. He told me that when he was young, they were poor and they did not have a piano. However, their kitchen table was made of boards covered with lino. He pushed the lino back and marked out the keys of a piano on the boards. He would finger the tunes on the imaginary piano and could hear the notes in his head. He then got his brass instrument and practiced with one hand and played the accompaniment on the imaginary piano with the other.

He was truly a gifted musician and brought much entertainment and joy to others. In Matthew 10:8 Jesus told His disciples "Freely you have received, freely give".

Reflection: Jesus, please show me how to give generously of the things that I do have; time, energy, talent, and prayer.

Smart Dark Horse

Obesity was not a problem as we grew up. Fresh food was usually grown locally and because there was no home refrigeration, the food was delivered frequently. Tinned food was only available from some overseas countries.

When my father transferred his business interests to dairy farming, things changed for us. We had no electricity, and our transport was by push bikes and horses. We were the last on the telephone line, so some of our neighbours, the closest two kilometres or a bit over one mile away, would walk over to us to make their phone calls.

All milk was sold fresh, so for our milk to be on the customers' tables for breakfast, the milking needed to be completed and at the vendor's pick-up point before 6 am. This meant that cows had to be moved to a closer paddock last thing at night and the cart horse had to be yarded ready to be harnessed for the morning delivery. It was the responsibility of us boys to catch the saddle horse and do the roundup ready for the morning.

Darkie, the saddle horse which came with the property, was as old as us but far more cunning. He would try to kick your foot out of the stirrup as you mounted. Once mounted, Darkie still thought he knew best. He was a great stock horse and could anticipate a beast's movement before we could. One evening my brother was bringing up the cart horse at top speed, but while Darkie was overtaking him, he crashed through a bush. Hidden in it was a stump on which he smashed my brother's shin bone. My brother then had to get off while the horse was galloping; making sure his other foot didn't become caught in the stirrup. Now on the ground, he started to crawl the half-mile or kilometre towards home, calling out as he went, with the foot of his injured leg dangling behind him.

One of our neighbours was coming through the paddocks with his lantern, to make a phone call, and heard my brother. When he found him, he told him to stay where he was while he got help. He hurried to our home where they phoned the ambulance, and Dad went back with a blanket to keep him warm and a lantern to show the ambulance where to locate the patient. In those days we rode our horses at top speed, but we only had one horse power. We did reckless things while still Primary School age, learning to be careful by our mistakes. By contrast, today's young people have multiple horse power, often travelling at top speed, sometimes causing injury.

My brother and I needed to pray the prayer in Psalm 25:7. "Remember not the sins of my youth, nor my transgressions: according to Thy mercy remember Thou me for Thy goodness' sake, O Lord."

Reflection: Father God, I thank you that you were able to keep my father safe during his youth and that he has been an effective instrument for you.

Small Beginnings

When my brother had a fall from a horse and broke his leg, he was admitted to hospital, where they set it and put it in plaster. After a few days, they noticed that it was not knitting correctly. It then had to be broken again and reset. He came home fitted with a steel stirrup, which enabled him to move about, but no horse or bike riding was allowed.

He was the mechanically minded one of the family, so to fill in his time, he took the shafts off the billy-cart and put wheels out in front, making it a Go-Kart. This was quite a job as there was no electricity, and holes had to be drilled by hand with brace and bits. These were hand turned drills, now only seen in Museums. Bolts and nuts were acquired from Dad's collection. The back wheels were cast iron from an old hand push lawn mower, the front ones were of unknown origin. In the beginning it was steered by ropes similar to driving a horse.

Brace & Bit

Next, he tried to use a steering wheel like those on a car. He could not get that to work efficiently. So, he fixed a joystick on the side, with a rod connecting the front wheels, which gave him good stable steering. Now it was power that he needed and achieved it by getting whoever could be persuaded to push him. With this stable steering he could now do sharp turns and broad sides. Every person is given opportunities to use the gifts with which they are born, and his were mechanical creations. As soon as he could leave school, he took an apprenticeship as a mechanic in which he excelled. He improved his skills by buying a doctor's stethoscope to detect any imperfect performance of the engines, which could not be picked up by the natural ear.

He didn't want to remain earth-bound, so he progressed to learning to fly, being required to pay his own way. The training planes were Tiger Moths which were used in those days. I asked him how he felt on his first flight. He said, "I was nervous until the engine started then I knew I was right". Years later, he flew around the Northern half of Australia, keeping the aircraft airworthy.

This was a long way from the Go-Kart. Often it is from small things that ambitions come, and with discipline and work the achievements become a reality.

Zechariah 4:10 says, Living Bible. "Do not despise this small beginning, for the eyes of the Lord rejoice to see the work begin."

Reflection: Lord Jesus, I thank you for the talents that you have given me, help me to use them even in the smallest ways to bring glory to you.

Boys will be Boys

Looking back, I am surprised at the things we were allowed to do at a young age. In the Depression days, I had my holidays at Uncle Edwards' farm. I enjoyed farm life so much that while I was staying there, I would rather stay on my own than go to town and run the risk of not being allowed to return to the farm.

Norm, 1934

When I was 10 years old, Uncle Eddy and his family went away for the day, and rather than leave me there on my own, they told me to walk over to Uncle Tom's farm about five kilometres away.

Things were hard on the land, which is often the case, but it was a great way of life, yet they often couldn't meet all their commitments. Uncle Eddy worked his farm plus two other farms, where the owners had to leave to find work elsewhere, to keep the banks happy.

I needed to walk past each of these two farmhouses but was forbidden to go near them. The owner of the first property must have had some severe emotional problems, because sometimes he would come back and wander around the place. Aunty would be anxious and keep the kids inside while he was about. I set out early in the morning for my walk to Uncle Tom's place. I passed the first house, then went two kilometres or a bit more than one mile on to the next one, where things were left just as they were when the owner walked off the property, curtains at the windows and furniture in place. All horse and hand powered machinery was properly parked in the sheds. I remember being quite sad at the sight of all this deserted property. I was too young, then, to understand the demands which banks made on adults.

I continued for the last two kilometres to Uncle Tom's place. There were no phones, but we just knew that I would be taken in and given a meal, and about 3 pm, I would be sent on my way back, to cover the five kilometre or just over three mile journey before dark. By then, Uncle and his family would be home. What I remember most about this particular trip was that Uncle Tom had lots of Kurrajongs which were great fodder trees. We called them 'Green Hay Stacks'. He had climbed a twelve-foot ladder up one of these tall trees in order to lop the leafy branches for his stock. My boyish mind got into action, and I started to remove the ladder, which I would have had no hope of putting back. From my Uncle's lofty position, he could see my intent, and in no uncertain language and tone, he told me to leave his ladder alone.

Surprise! Surprise! I did leave the ladder there and was instructed that as the branches fell, I was to spread them around so that all the stock could get a share.

In this way, I gained my Uncle's approval and experienced Proverb 22:15 which reads "Foolishness is bound up in the heart of a child, but the rod of correction will drive it far from him". It was the opportunity to be independent and adventurous and the development of relationships not the multitude of goods or toys which made my childhood educational and fulfilling.

Reflection: Oh Lord, what a variety of ways you use to teach us the lessons of life. I thank you for your grace and kindness in our lives.

Two Lessons

Droving sheep and cattle is a practice of the past, except in times of drought, when the stock travel along stock routes for feed. In my early years, there was no 'stock road transport'. The stock were moved by walking them from place to place or to the railheads to be transported by train.

The father of one of my friends was a stock dealer and often had sheep on the road, moving them from the place of purchase to the new owner. Sometimes a mob would be shorn at his shearing shed and then sold on.

Once, he needed to move a small mob of a few hundred, just a day's distance away. Rather than try to find a drover, he told his son to "get Norm" (we were both still in Primary school) to come out, get a horse each and move the sheep. The friend came to town, stayed the night, and we were to ride our push bikes out early the next morning, to get the horses and be back ready to start the job at daybreak. We planned to start at 5 am. We were quite excited at being given such a responsibility.

We woke, thinking it was five minutes to 5 am, left quietly, riding our bikes out, catching the horses, and riding back ready for the day of droving. When we arrived back, it was still long before 5 am. In the dark, we had looked at the big clock in the sitting room and mistaken the time. It was 25 minutes past 11 pm not five minutes to 5 a.m. So, we were grounded until it was time to go for the sheep.

This was mistake number one for the day. Lesson one was 'Don't be hasty, but look carefully before you act.'

Mistake number two was; we did not take enough water for the day and by mid-day we were out of that necessary fluid. To this day, I could go to the place where there was an empty house, and we found a tank with water in it. We experienced that wonderful feeling of quenching our thirst, filling our containers, and learning Lesson Number two, 'Take plenty of water, prepare properly whatever you are doing'.

Selected passages from the book of Isaiah 43:19-20 say "I will even make a way in the wilderness and rivers in the desert, to give drink to my people".

Reflection: Thank you Lord for all the answers that you provide for all those who love and serve you.

Teaching a Young Dog

When I visited a property the other day, I noticed a sign saying, "Beware of the geese". It reminded me of a happening in my early days on the farm. We had three geese and a large white gander. The offspring were an acceptable addition to meals on special occasions.

The old land line phones were the quick connection to the outside world, and neighbours drove farm vehicles or walked over the paddocks to use our phone as it was the last on the line.

One afternoon, a neighbour arrived with his new cattle dog on the back of his truck. He was a beautiful dog, about eighteen months old and still learning. On their property, they had poultry and no other dogs, so he was king of his farm yard, and had not encountered geese before. When the farmer went into the house to make his phone call, the dog jumped off the truck to investigate this new farm and headed straight for the big white gander, The gander stretched out his neck and made the appropriate noises, of which our dogs took good warning. The new chum however kept on going, the gander attacked the dog, catching him above the eye, held on and proceeded to belt him with his wings.

Geese. Photo courtesy of Kelly Scriven

There was much yelping, dust flying as the dog struggled to get away, but the gander held on. When at last he freed himself, blood streaming from above his eye, he jumped back to his place of safety on the back of the truck. Afterwards, during the many visits to our place, he never left the truck. The intelligence of the dog was obvious, he was teachable.

In life, we should ask God as the Psalmist did in Psalm 119:65-66. "Thou has dealt well with Thy servant, O Lord, according unto Thy Word. Teach me good judgment and knowledge:"

Reflection: Father I thank you for those experiences that I don't particularly enjoy because I know that the lessons I will learn will be valuable.

Advice to live by

When I think of how my parents influenced me in the things of life, I recall mother gave me lots of advice.

One important piece was "If you are persuaded by your mind, or dominated by another mind, without it touching your emotions, it is usually not good. If something moves your emotions only, then you are likely to make bad decisions. If your mind carries your judgment and your heart is warmed, you are much more likely to make better decisions".

My father's influence came more by his actions and the way he applied himself. He ran his boot making business and was very successful. His rule was 'A good article, a good price and a good service'. To achieve this, only those who knew him well realized that he often worked until 11 pm doing the finer work, while mother read to him books of achievement. (No tape recorders in those days). In this way he also kept his mind active and motivated.

He was a musician and held to position of Solo cornet for years in a brass band of up to forty players. He never missed a weekly, two hourly, band practice or public engagement. He set aside a given time each day for practice. When he felt he was getting too old, and holding that position could hinder a younger player, he resigned, giving them the opportunity he'd had.

He went dairy farming and applied that same diligence to his new way of life. He started at the bottom and in seven years, although he did not own the biggest herd, he had the highest production per cow and top-quality milk.

When I went into business, he gave me the same advice which had served him so well, and said, "I will advise you, but you must do it yourself, make your own mistakes and learn from them". This certainly helped me to be successful and later, a larger business bought me out.

When I came to the Ministry, those same rules applied. 'Make sure your presentation of the Gospel is understandable, work at it even when others stop and remember that you are there to serve, not to be served'.

My parents' example was great. Jesus Christ's example was perfect, and I am still trying to improve. The Bible says in Philippians 4:7, "The peace of God, which surpasses all understanding, will guard your hearts and minds through Christ Jesus". And in verse 13, "I can do all things through Christ who strengthens me".

Reflection: Lord I thank you for the example of those that you have brought across my path every day but help me to discern what is good and not so good.

Pink Sheets

The medical health care which we enjoy today is different from when my father's family was being established. The first and second children of that family died of diphtheria. There were three more girls born before my father came into the world. With a mother and three older sisters to do the housekeeping, as an only son, he was spoilt.

At an early age, he got what they termed 'Inflammation of the bowel'. I understand now that was probably appendicitis. They expected him to die from it. He told me that he did not remember how long he was unaware of what was going on around him, but when he became conscious, he could feel his ribs protruding as if they could easily break through his skin. It was a wonder he lived! However, his small stature was attributed to that illness and he also lost a year's schooling.

He learned his trade and owned his own business before he married. After marriage, if my mother was away, if any housework or cooking that was required, his sisters would come to his rescue. Eventually his sisters married and moved away. I, being the eldest was shown how to carry on with the housekeeping, that is, how to cook, which was done on a wood stove. I did not cook cakes and the like, but was able to provide a working man's meal of meat, vegetables, and sweets.

Then the cleaning! When mother was due home, Dad expected everything to be up to her expected standard, no dirty dishes, linen, or clothes about. That is where I made my big mistake. I had been shown how to boil the copper, sort the clothes which would boil and not lose their colour, rinse in cold water, except the whites which had to have a blue bag added to the last rinse. Dad did not know how, and had no intention of learning. He wanted the result, so I had to produce it.

Cooking went well enough; everyone was satisfied and well fed. The washing up was done in a wash-up dish on the table, put into a tray and dried with a tea towel.

The sheets in those days were all white, so when it came to the washing, I somehow put some red articles in the copper with the sheets. The colour ran and the sheets came out pink. We were years ahead of the accepted style of today's coloured linen. There was nothing for it, but to face the mistake as there was certainly no way of hiding it. But after all these years, in my mind's eye, I can still visualise pink sheets which should have been white, hanging on the clothes line at the old home.

The memory of the pink sheets does not hinder my sleep. I try to practice the Bible verses of Psalm 63:6-7. "When I remember Thee upon my bed, and meditate on Thee in the night watches, because Thou hast been my help, therefore in the shadow of Thy wings will I rejoice".

Reflection: Jesus please help me not to lose sleep over the trivial things in life but keep me from treating eternal things as trivial.

Washing Copper - Photo courtesy of Kilkivan Museum Queensland

Retraining

One of my earliest experiences of the intelligence of horses came at about age eleven. During the Depression, my father needed to sell his horse and gear, to get enough money to keep his business afloat. He had a reputation for his abilities with animals. A friend bought a horse for his delivery service. He was a beautiful young horse which gave promise of many years of work, but had been poorly broken in. The owner asked my father if he would re-train him.

This was when my learning experience about horses began. First, the horse needed to be ridden and taught to respond to the reins, because he had not been properly mouthed. When he was mounted, he would just stand and when we tried to move him forward, he would rear straight up and remain in that position. He was the only horse I have experienced that could do this and not fall. One needed to hold on to his mane or slide off his tail. He would do the same whenever we tried to turn him left or right.

My father put me in the saddle, got behind, hit him on the rump to move him forward and then he would come down. It was slow progress and was weeks before I could give him a two- or three-mile workout after school. However, if you tried to turn him, stop, or change direction he would rear again. We used various methods until he gradually became quite reliable.

The next thing was to teach him to pull a cart, taking different routes with stops and starts. This was achieved fairly quickly as we had already been working him. He went on to give his owners valuable service for years, until they changed to motor vehicles.

When our family moved to the farm, we broke in a number of horses, children's ponies which became very reliable, stock horses which could cut a beast out of a mob with ease and draught-horses that surprised us by what they could pull, given the right training.

We had an ex-trotter who became a sulky horse and was a delight to drive.

There is a big difference between animals and people. People will not change their bad ways unless there is a personal desire to change or an awareness of their need to find real fulfillment.

In Acts 3:19, the Living Bible says "Now change your minds and attitude to God and turn to Him so He can cleanse away your sins and send you wonderful times of refreshment from the presence of the Lord".

Reflection: Thank you my loving Father, for the way that you are making me grow, day by day, by the power of your spirit.

Family the Great Gift

When I was growing up, the Christmas gifts that were given usually had a small monetary value. All the relatives would meet and what we had was each other's love and friendship. There was no going away for holidays, just visiting each other's places for a few days.

The Family 1977
Jean Helen, Norm, Jean, Olwyn, Alan, Ian, Lionel

Now I realize that family is the greatest gift. Today, with family planning made easy, fewer children is the "in thing".

My wife and I had five children and they are one of our greatest joys. On one occasion, we went to a village Church, all seven of us, where we were able to worship and thank God for our many gifts. The Service over, we were moving out and passed a lady with one child only, a 12-year-old girl. As I was last of our group, I heard the girl say in an almost startled voice, "Mum I thought they'd never stop coming". She obviously found such numbers very different.

Family planning is not new, for the greatest gift, God's Son, was planned. The Bible says in Luke 1:30-32 "And the angel said... 'Fear not Mary: for thou hast found favour with God.... behold thou shalt conceive in thy womb, and bring forth a son, and shalt call his name JESUS. He shall be great and shall be called the Son of the Highest'". And in Matthew 1:21 "for He shall save His people from their sins".

Reflection: Lord I thank you for my family no matter how strange we may look to others.

Last Request.

When AIDS became a dreaded disease, it was often preached as the wrath of God for sin upon gay men. At this time, treatment was not available. Fortunately, today there is treatment. In our large cities there were beds for the dying, mostly young men. Lots of families did not want to know or visit them. They often died alone.

One of the most touching acts of friendship and kindness that expressed the love of Jesus I've heard, comes out of this loneliness.

A friend, a heroin addict, went out to see a man we will call Luke. He is one in a row of young men fading away in their beds, knowing they would die. The two friends sit on the veranda – Luke has a blanket around him and he still shivers. His friend asks "What is your favourite colour?"

"Blue" was the reply. On leaving, the addict walks the street asking for money from anyone who would give, for a dressing gown. Many refused but some gave. Driven on by the need of a friend, dying and cold, the impossible was achieved, seventy dollars. When the shop attendant at David Jones was told, it was for a special person, she gift-wrapped it and the chenille gown made a large parcel.

The parcel was presented to Luke in his row of distressed young men. He struggles to unwrap the parcel. He is weak, so the nurse and friend help him put it on. The gaunt face shines, someone cares, and the smile will be remembered for ever as the tears ran down his cheeks. "I think I'll take it with me". The Authorities tell the friend that that could be arranged. Within days he dies. He goes in his blue dressing gown. His family did not want to know but the friend attended to his last requests.

Jesus said in Matthew Chapter 25 – "Come, ye blessed of my Father, inherit the kingdom prepared for you........ I was a stranger and you took me in: naked and you clothed me: sick, and ye visited me".

Reflection: Thank you for those strangers who have crossed our paths and helped us in small and big ways.

Learning from the Trees

Kurrajong Tree

The marvel of trees has been a great education for me. As I left school early at thirteen, I soon realised my learning could come from the older men in my life; the drovers, cattle men, fencing contractors, swaggies, and retired land holders.

I soon discovered that trees and where they grew provided lots of information about their uses. There were ways of telling those which would make good sawn timber or good fence posts. Others indicated there was water below or provided fodder for stock, which were called green haystacks by the old timers. Still others signposted rich soil, moisture-holding soil, and there are trees which improve the soil. It was, and still is, an absorbing education.

In my early days at school there were poems about trees and we must have had a teacher who was protesting, so there's nothing new. We were encouraged to protest about Sandalwood being exported to Asia. I was to see the beautiful, aromatic wood years later, while working along the Mooney River. It had durability that meant thin fence posts lasted longer than steel posts. When boiling the billy, we looked for sandalwood because it burnt hot and the scent was wonderful. We could see the oil dripping out of it.

News releases tell me now they are growing sandalwood commercially. It sometimes takes a while for us to realise all the good and profitable things we have. It is important not to lose the values which make for happy living, for we will have to learn it all over again if we forget.

Deuteronomy 4:9 says, " Only take heed to thyself, and keep thy soul diligently, lest thou forget the things which thine eyes have seen, and lest they depart from thy heart all the days of thy life: but teach them thy sons and thy sons' sons."

Reflection: Father I thank you for the way that we can learn from the natural world that you created.

Father's Call Home

My father had learned the boot trade during the times when parents were required to pay an amount for the first twelve months for an employer to take on an apprentice. He later had his own successful business, before taking his skills on to the land and becoming a company director of an associated business.

In retirement he and my mother toured the east and north of Australia for some years, seeing and experiencing many of the places Dad's old customers had talked about. Many of these experiences were recorded in photography.

People who live long lives often have many friends and associates who suffer sickness, trials, and sorrow. My parents were great visitors of such people, standing by them in their need.

One of Dad's business associates had retired to the coast and tragedy had struck them. One of their children committed suicide. Dad and Mum drove hundreds of kilometres to be with them. A fortnight later they were returning home in their new Ford Falcon station wagon. Coming up the Dorrigo Range, the Ford started to boil. Dad pulled over on to a lookout for the car to cool down. There was a good view and Dad said, "I'll go and get the camera". He was a long time returning and when Mother looked around, he had opened the car door, but had collapsed from a massive heart attack. Mother applied mouth to mouth and a passing nurse continued, but it was too late.

The car had never boiled before or since. Can you imagine what could have happened on that Range if he had been driving?

I believe the Scripture which says in Psalm 91:11, "He will give His angels charge over thee to keep thee in all thy ways".

Reflection: Lord help me to remember that even in my darkest days, You are in control of, not only our world, but the whole of history.

The last photo taken of Wilfred & Elvie Morris before Wilfred was called home to glory

Home on a Wing and a Prayer

The personalities in families are very different and our family was no exception. I was farm orientated, my brother was mechanically minded, and my two sisters, wonderful girls, had their special gifts which they used in their careers and later in their homes and families.

Once I had got over an early childhood fear of aeroplanes, I became aware that planes were the way of the future. My brother had achieved his mechanics qualifications and was given foreman's responsibilities. He was then looking for new challenges, so I encouraged him to get his pilot's licence. As the aerodrome joined our property, we saw the Tiger Moths regularly, and he started training as time and money was available.

Hilton Morris in the cockpit of an aeroplane –
Photo courtesy Wilga Morris & Valarie Barker

One day, doing a trial cross country flight, he was about forty miles out when the motor missed a beat. His mechanical knowledge sent his anxiety level up so he returned to base by the most direct route, put the plane down, and without any ado, parked it in the hanger. Tiger Moths had two magnetos. The next morning when the instructor arrived to start the plane, one magneto fell out and the other wasn't working. It was wonderful for my brother to realize that he had escaped disaster by his prompt action in returning immediately. 'He was home on a wing and a prayer'.

He experienced what the Bible says in Psalm 91:11-12. "He shall give His angels charge over thee, to keep thee in all thy ways. They shall bear thee up in their hands, lest thou dash thy foot against a stone".

Reflection: Father how great are you to make each and every one of us differently and give each of us our own special gifts.

Keeping Silent

Having gained his pilot's licence, my brother flew small planes under varying conditions in the north of Australia for years, experiencing greater safety as the planes improved. On one occasion he was bringing a new plane from the south, having one of his superiors as a passenger. His boss was in for a new experience. They left Alice Springs for Darwin, flying at a high altitude with the instruments working well. He and his passenger were enjoying the benefits of this updated aircraft.

Suddenly the cockpit filled with smoke. He realised that it was probably an electrical fault, so he switched off the instrument panel. Their enjoyment turned to anxious waiting to see if the smoke cleared, which gradually, it did. This proved that he had made the right decision. He now descended to a lower altitude, going back to the old method of flying by sight and landmarks.

He found and followed the highway but was wondering how he was going to notify Tenant Creek that he was in trouble and would need to land there? He thought, "I'll take the risk, switch on the radio, tell them we have a fire in the electrical system and are coming in for a manual landing." The radio came back to life; he gave his message and switched it off again without too much smoke.

When the runway came into sight, there was a fire engine and ambulance waiting. As he put down, the emergency services raced along each side of the landing strip. Climbing out of the plane, he thanked the emergency men for their presence. They replied, "This is all new gear and we've been waiting for a trial run."

Till now, his boss had not spoken. Now he asked my brother if he was nervous. My brother's response was, "No time for that, I was too busy making decisions about flying the plane". His boss responded with, "My hands are all sweaty". He no doubt learned that when your life depends on another, you need the ability to not talk. The Bible says, "Do you want to be counted wise, to build a reputation for wisdom? Here's what you do: Live well, live wisely, live humbly. It's the way you live, not the way you talk, that counts."

Reflection: Father help me to remember that sometimes I can be a greater blessing to someone by being silent.

A Missing Brother

One of our long-time friends came from a large family of nine children. Times were often hard, yet they made their fun and enjoyment from ordinary things, because their parents could not give them what today would be called 'the best start in life'. However, they had lots of love which made them rich in character, and as they left home and made their separate ways in life, they became good citizens. Because of their background they knew and cared about each other and their achievements. This circle was broken when one brother left with no forwarding address or contact number.

Years later, a nephew, travelling in a remote part of Australia, was stopped at road works and saw a man who looked like one of his uncles. He approached him, asking if his name was '-------' using his missing uncle's name. The man gave a different name. The nephew said, "You look like one of my uncles. I thought you might be his brother".

He was so impressed by the resemblance that when he came home, he shared the experience with the rest of the family. In the following years he would often talk about his experience by the road works, being so taken with the family likeness of the road worker. The family were still wondering what had become of their brother.

One day the news came that he had passed away. A mate living in that remote village of Australia knew him by another name, and going through his few personal belongings, found his real identity and notified his family. They were at a loss to understand why he had removed himself from the circle of family love and care, yet were relieved that they had at last found their lost brother and that he had lived into senior years.

We may escape from our family connections, but the Bible tells of God's perfect knowledge of man. In Psalm 139:7-8 we read

"Whither shall I go from Thy Spirit? or whither shall I flee from Thy presence? If I ascend up into Heaven, Thou art there: if I make my bed in hell, behold, Thou art there".

Reflection: Father I thank you that it won't matter how lost we get, You, will always know exactly where we are and what we need.

Dreams

People have dreams, ambitions, and purpose. Some are promoted by sellers of something they tell us that we can "Take home and pay for later". Others start out but do not count on the amount of effort needed to achieve it.

No hill is climbed without continued effort. Sometimes, when people don't get what they thought was their dream, for whatever reason, they give up and live unfulfilled lives. I have met many such people in a mining town, for they seem to arrive there hoping to find a dream or fulfillment without the required effort.

One day a Scottish man invited me to his home which was one of the better homes in the town. When I arrived, his wife and his teenage children greeted me graciously. He said, "I want to present you with a book." I suspected he had a drinking problem that was not obvious to everyone. He gave me the book entitled "Alcoholics Anonymous". He had autographed the front page and said "I have no more use for it, I have not been able to abstain from the drink, and it's got me and is a problem to me". I tried to encourage him to try again, but it was plain that his hope was gone.

He then brought out a magazine from years before with a feature article of a young Scottish man with a number of camels who had come to Australia to spread the Gospel in the outback. This was the same man. Had the constant travelling, the spiritual care of the people and isolation in our great country taken its toll? He came with purpose, but somewhere he lost it. How sad!

Somewhere in between his losing hope and my visit he had written a poem for the Queen's Coronation. It was acknowledged by her Majesty, and I found it when I opened the book. Now, I was sitting in his home and receiving the book, while he indicated that he had lost purpose and hope. At such times I felt that any words of mine were very inadequate.

He needed to realize that God specializes in giving purpose and hope, but we have to ask Him. Matthew 7:7-8 says "Ask, and it will be given to you; seek, and you will find; knock, and it will be opened to you. For everyone who asks receives, and he who seeks finds, and to him who knocks it will be opened".

Reflection: Thank you Lord God that we can come to you particularly when we feel things are hopeless.

Modern Living

Recently my wife and I spent an extended weekend in the hospitality of a family unit consisting of a husband, wife, four children and a Nan. The home consisted of four bedrooms, rumpus room, deck, ample granny flat where Nan lived, and a large backyard. There was plenty of room for the kids, a computer with the relevant accessories, and three cars. The husband has a full-time job, and the wife works part-time. Their recreation time revolves around bike riding, cricket, football, swimming, and music. It all sounds great! How we enjoyed our stay and also learnt something more of the modern pressures of life.

Their week turned out to be quite busy as on the first day Nan had a car prang and the car would be off the road for 3 weeks. On day two, the 11-year-old had his first orthodontic treatment and had a sore mouth. This was followed by day three when the seven-year-old lost a front tooth and wanted attention. Finally, to wrap up the busy week on day four found the nine-year-old fell in the evening and at 7 pm was taken to the hospital, where an X-Ray showed a break in her arm. They arrived home about 10 p.m. with the child's arm in a plaster from the hand to above the elbow.

The need of all the children at this time is not things, but love and to be made feel special. This is what is important; the inner person's health helps the outer problems to heal and assists in their stable growing up.

> For our hosts, the old saying applies –
> "The young look forward,
> The old look back.
> And the middle-aged look tired".

What impressed us was the fact that the family stayed focused on living well and only saw things as a means of enjoying life and helping inner health.

A great lesson for us old folk was that this family has the spiritual values which help in making good choices, thus building good characters. They have to constantly remind themselves of the truth in Matthew 16:26 "For what is a man profited, if he shall gain the whole world, and lose his own soul? For what shall a man give in exchange for his soul?"

Reflection: Father help us to remember no matter how busy we get, if we look to you, you will be able to give us the strength, courage, and means to get things done.

Alive and Kicking

Our first child was born out west in Mt. Isa. The poor child! She had to survive new parents who were learning on her. Love was plentiful but the best intentions, good desires and much reading did not exclude us from mistakes. Some of our circumstances included heat, mosquitoes, red dust spreading its film everywhere, and lack of fresh food for mother.

Mosquito nets had two purposes: firstly, they were supposed to keep mosquitoes out. If any part of the body was out from under the net, it would certainly be covered with mosquito bites. Secondly, we had an electrical table fan, made of all metal and with only one speed in those days. By keeping the net wet and using the fan to blow through it, we kept the baby cooler. She needed lots of boiled water to prevent dehydration.

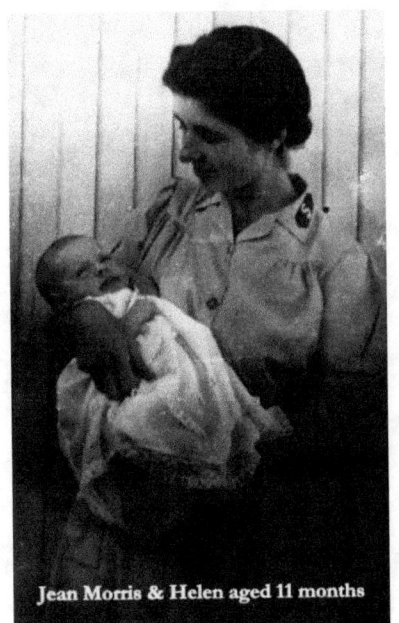
Jean Morris & Helen aged 11 months

Lack of good food for her mother meant that breast milk was inadequate, causing constipation troubles for the baby. Someone gave us the advice to soak wheatgerm in water and give her the water, which solved the problem. I am thankful for the God given resourcefulness of Mother's love and care which overcame many challenges.

We hear people speak of the 'good old days', but others refer to them as 'those trying times'. Therefore, we all need God's help as in Psalm 145:18-19 (Moffatt's Translation) "The Eternal is near all who call on Him, who call on Him sincerely; He satisfies His worshippers, He hears their cry and helps them."

Reflection: Father I am eternally grateful that you knew what you were doing with my life when you provided me these wonderful people to love me.

Thief

Over 50 years ago, families in the West had goats which provided milk and they became attached to their owners. One of my Minister friends at Longreach had a goat which he had trained to come when he called her. The town's folk milked their goats in the morning. When they let them out, they would all join together as a mob and go out on the flats to graze for the day, going home to their separate owners at night.

Sometimes my friend had to go out of town for an Evening Service or function, often up to two hundred kilometres or more away. He would need to leave after lunch. Therefore, to prevent the goat returning home and becoming a nuisance to the neighbours before his return in the late evening, he would go to the flats and call his goat. He would open the back door of his vehicle; the goat would jump in and be taken home to be penned up in her shelter. In the morning she would be ready to be milked and he knew she would not have been going astray in the neighbourhood while he was away until late.

One morning, for some unknown reason, his goat did not go out to the flats with the others. My Minister friend went down town to carry out some business and while walking along the street, he saw his goat, in a hurry, coming out of the shop where vegies were sold, with a cauliflower in her mouth. She saw him and enthusiastically followed him, so all could see that he was her owner. He told me "I hurriedly went to my car and opened the back door. She jumped in still holding the cauliflower in her mouth. I quickly took her back to her shelter for the remainder of the day". He then had to visit the scene of the crime, confess his goat's theft, and put things right with the proprietor.

In Proverbs 16:7-8 we read, "When you please the Lord, He can make your enemies into friends. It is better to have a little, honestly earned, then to have a large income, gained dishonestly".

Reflection: Father please give me strength to always be honest because you can see everything that I do.

Commitment

In our senior years we have experienced a wonderful quality of life thanks to the dedication of medical professionals and the wonders of new technical procedures. Seventy or more years ago, the facilities we enjoy now were not available, but the commitment of doctors and staff was just as great. This is one story which was passed down to me:

The weather was very wet. The young family was isolated on a farm surrounded by black mud. The young wife suffered a miscarriage and her husband could not get her out. So, he went by horse until he could phone a doctor. The doctor replied "Go back and get a horse and cart and meet me at the end of the all-weather road. I'll bring the necessary equipment, transfer to the cart and you can take me to the farm. I'll do a curette or whatever is necessary at your cottage."

I'm told that this is what happened: When they arrived, the doctor said to the husband, "You will be my theatre nurse, looking after the anaesthetic and following my instructions." The operation over and the patient recovering, it was a case of getting the doctor and his instruments back into the horse and cart, through the miles of mud to the all-weather road, the doctor back to his own practice in town and the farmer back to his needy wife. That couple lived to celebrate over sixty years of marriage.

The commitment of the doctor, the husband and wife resulted in a good outcome.

God also requires commitment in Psalm 37:5 says "Commit thy way unto the Lord; trust also in Him; and He shall bring it to pass".

Reflection: God, I thank you that when we need a solution to a particular problem, you have a solution even if it is unusual.

Under New Management

Fifty odd years ago, marriage services were more important than they are today. Marriages then were expected to last, but even so, there were still some partnerships which made people think they were 'uneven matches.'

Norm & Jean Morris on their Wedding Day

When I managed to convince my wife to marry me, it was considered by some to be that kind of 'uneven match'. My wife was competent in her own right academically and had a sweet personality, but I had left formal school at 13 years of age, worked among real men, been in business and wandered around the country, travelling light with no one to consider.

When I passed the entry to the Ministry, many considered it an "act of God". My study days were marked by challenging the lecturers on matters which I felt, in my short experience, did not work out in life.

When it was known that I was to marry my wife, whom others thought was out of my league, they questioned, "Would it work?" We married in Brisbane City. I had put my car in a secure parking lot to save our belongings being loaded with confetti and extras as country guests coming to the city were likely to do all manner of things, such as padlocking a chain and cow bell to the axle which they quite often did in our country town. The city police would not let that pass.

When the car driver was told, after the Reception, to take us to our car, he let some of my mates know where our car was, and they beat us to the car park. They bribed the management but were only allowed to put a large sign on the back 'UNDER NEW MANAGEMENT'. We had to travel through the city, till we were out of the traffic before we were able to remove the sign.

The new management of my gracious lady has knocked some of the rough edges off, but it has been a good journey for me.

In the spiritual world, Charles Gabriel expressed what new management was like in the Hymn:

"What a wonderful change in my life has been wrought Since Jesus came into my heart.
I have light in my soul for which long I had sought, Since Jesus came into my heart.
I have ceased from my wandering and going astray, Since Jesus came into my heart.
And my sins which were many are all washed away; Since Jesus came into my heart."

Reflection: Oh, Father God how great it is to know that we are all under new management once we ask you to come into our hearts, even if the changes take longer than we think they should.

The Last Cup of Coffee

In an ordinary house, in an ordinary country town, a farmer went to his front gate, but then decided to go back to the kitchen and have another cup of coffee with his wife.

They had started their marriage in the horse and sulky days in the south. He was successful in the rural scene, had made modifications to machinery which were patented, participated in Agricultural Politics and was a successful businessman.

Moving to Queensland, he saw the potential of growing wheat west of Goondiwindi, took up a block and became successful. The good large crop needed to be harvested, so he hired a contractor to do the job, who, with lights on the new harvester, worked through the night. The surrounding graziers flew their planes over each morning to see what the newcomer was doing next. His wife had supported him over all those years.

They enjoyed the coffee together. The photo on the wall showed eight children who were doing well in their chosen careers. They had had two deaths in the family, but their love for each other remained strong, during hardships, relocating to new communities, starting new adventures and the sorrows and joys of life. The farmer left the kitchen to go to his block, neither of them realizing that within hours he would be dead.

The Lord said in Revelation 2:10. "Be thou faithful unto death and I will give thee a crown of life."

Reflection: Lord I thank you that you know the number of my days. Help me to make the most of each day that I wake up for.

Guest Speaker

This story was printed in the first edition of this book in 2015.

Olwyn Harris - my sister

In 1979, Mrs Trevor Harris, then Olwyn Morris, attended the Gympie High School and no one could have predicted her achievements of the next thirty years. She did General Nursing at the Gympie General Hospital, her Midwifery at Toowoomba, and a degree of Bachelor of Nursing. She gained a Certificate in Business Administration, a Certificate in Training and Assessment, a Certificate in Christian Ministry and is the author of two published books. At the time of writing her position is "Injury Prevention and Management Specialist" in a national role. Trevor and Olwyn have four children and were at the time living in Toowoomba.

The Bible says of a good wife, in Proverbs 31:26-28 "She opens her mouth with wisdom, and on her tongue is the law of kindness. She watches over the ways of her household, and does not eat the bread of idleness. Her children rise up and call her blessed; her husband also, and he praises her." Olwyn was the Guest Speaker at The Union Church, Gympie, on Sunday 8th March, 2009.

Reflection: Lord I thank you for the blessing of my beautiful sister.

As Olwyn continues to grow and achieve, here are her own words about her life so far.

When you leave school, how do you make life determining decisions with any degree of discernment? It seems like an impossible undertaking. I remember sitting, filling out a form for university entry and thinking... "I would like to do Occupational Therapy. I would like to do Social Work. I would like to... so many options." I had the grades... but not the confidence. I was accepted into the nursing-school at the local hospital, one of the very last intakes before the program went to university. I also did midwifery... again one of the very last intakes before the program went tertiary. I worked right up until I took maternity leave, and then after my eldest daughter was born, went back to apply for work at the hospital because the economic downturn meant my husband's engineering degree was not so attractive on the employment market.

I sat in that interview and the Director of Nursing said to me... "So many women are not satisfied with just staying home to be a mother. I understand why you want to come back to professional work." I left that interview with a job and very angry.

My ambition at that time to *was* to be a mother, and I felt cheated that I would be working with other people's children, not my own. I also felt that this person had minimised my desire to be a stay-at-home parent. Years down the track and four children later, my ambition to be a stay-at-home mother was fulfilled... right up until my youngest daughter started fulltime school.

I completed my Bachelor of Nursing and was offered a job working as an "Injury Prevention and Management Specialist" in a national role in the mining industry... a role often filled by occupational therapists. I completed a Master of Counselling... where I work with vulnerable families and offer relationship counselling... a role undertaken by social workers. And into that mix, I studied a diploma in Christian Ministry... and I have a role as a pastor in a small rural church. I also have had six novels published since 2019: I love writing Australian historical fiction with a faith-based backdrop.

The Bible says in Psalms 37:4 "Take delight in the LORD, and he will give you the desires of your heart."
Sometimes it looks like those dreams and desires are far away... but looking back, I can see God never minimised any one of them; there is not one of those heart felt desires that God has withheld.

Sometimes he is not keeping dreams *from* us... but keeping them *for* us.

Reflection: Lord, what dreams and desires of my heart are you still holding for me?

Olwyn Harris' published novels:

A Snake and a Cat

Animals are great company. Dogs are so forgiving and very loyal. Cats are too! Cats have a special ability to get their own way, finding the sunniest spot and the softest cushion, but, I think, they can also be quite demanding, making you aware that they have needs you should meet. One of the most resourceful ladies we know enjoyed her kitten. One evening she heard it crying in a very distressed state. On investigating, she found a carpet snake making a meal of her kitten, hind legs first. This animal lover didn't want to kill the snake, but certainly wanted to rescue her pet. She caught the snake just below the head and held on very tightly until the snake, experiencing the treatment it gives to its prey, that of being crushed, released the cat's hind legs. The snake was then taken well out of harm's way and released. What courage and what kindness this lady showed. When I saw the kitten later, it had made a full recovery.

I have to wonder if those of us who have had loved ones hurt, would be as forgiving and kind as my resourceful friend? Jesus taught in Matthew 5:44 "But I say unto you, love your enemies, bless those who curse you, do good to those who hate you, and pray for those who spitefully use you and persecute you."

Reflection: Oh, Jesus help me to remember that you love those who hurt and hate me, help me to follow your example by forgiving them.

Buying a Shack

Stock and Station agents, while selling real estate, meet a variety of personalities. In my home town one morning, one of the leading agents had such an experience.

In walked a senior man, dressed in his clean, but well-worn riding britches, shirt, and his R.M. Williams boots. Sun tan showed he had spent many years in the sun, and when he shook hands, they revealed callouses which were the result of lots of hard manual work. His opening greeting was, "I have decided to retire in this area and want to buy a shack. Can you show me some?"

The agent was glad to help and collected a list of properties for sale in the poorer end of town. He showed him a number of them, but they were not the kind of shack the man wanted. In fact, he did not even go inside most of them. He wanted to see more, so back to the office for another list of houses in the upper end of town. None of the properties suited him, or were too close to neighbours.

By lunch time the agent had exhausted his list of prospects. He said to the client, "Go have some lunch, and I will see if I can find anything else for you to look at, be back by 2 pm."

At 2 p.m. when our man from the west turned up, the agent said, "I can only find one more place for you to look at. It's a little out of town, a big brick home on 25 acres and fairly expensive." The sunburnt client said, "We'd better have a look at it." When they drove on to the property, got out and had a look around, the buyer said, "Just the shack I want." The agent learned never to judge a book by its cover, because this man was a well-heeled or prosperous grazier.

He lived for years, a quiet life in this large home, with a few well cared for cattle on the acreage and no neighbours to bother him. When it comes to Heavenly housing, Jesus said in the Gospel of

John 14:2-3: "In my Father's house are many mansions; if it were not so, I would have told you. I go to prepare a place for you. And if I go and prepare a place for you, I will come again and receive you to myself; that where I am, there you may be also."

Reflection: God, I thank you that, no matter what our circumstances are here on earth, if we love you, we have a mansion waiting for us in Heaven.

Fake or Real

Visiting is one practice that is disappearing from many people's communication skills. These days, it's done more by 'phone, when you hear but do not see' or the latest is 'phone when you can see and hear.'

What wonders the new technology brings! Those emails where you do not hear or see, just read. Many of our youth use texting, where with just as few letters as possible it is conceivable to convey the message.

I am aware that visiting, enjoying people, their presence, expressions, and conversation in their own environment makes for a fulfilling experience, which supersedes the modern methods of communication, wonderful as they are!

I visited a widow who had had her trials and successes, is very able, makes an impact in her circle and is loved by her friends. She has artistic talents, keeping her home welcoming, her lawn neat with well-placed statues, gardens bare of weeds and pot plants hanging for the best effect. The overall colours seem to complement each other. On one visit, I noticed a colourful flower which stood out from the rest.

I asked, where did you get that plant? Her smile made me take a closer look and she said "It is artificial". I realized it had no life in it; it was a fake, even though it set off the appearance of the garden. I felt a leaf to prove that my eyes were not deceiving me and realized that I needed to improve my discernment.

I am glad that God is all-seeing and knows when we are real. His advice in 2 Timothy 3:4-5 says of some people, they are "lovers of pleasure rather than lovers of God, having a form of godliness but denying its power. From such people turn away".

Reflection: Please Lord, teach me to be real.

God's Comfort

There was a period when I supplemented our income by working part-time at an engineering works in a small country town. Their jobs ranged from making steel cattle yards to keeping the local cattle transport company trucks on the road. The owner was a capable and resourceful man. The hard jobs were done straight away; the impossible ones took a little longer.

One morning my wife came to the shop and I could tell that something was wrong. She had received a phone call to say my father had died while they were half way up the Dorrigo Range and mother was in the Dorrigo hospital. It appeared they needed me to identify my father and pick up my mother.

This is how it happened. Dad and Mum had gone over to the coast to be with some long-time friends who had suffered a sudden and traumatic bereavement. After their friends were able to come to terms with their loss a little, Dad and Mum, in their new model Ford Falcon, started back to their inland home and were coming up the Dorrigo Range when the car started to boil. It had never overheated before and never did again during the years afterwards that my mother drove that car.

Dad pulled over to a rest area and went to look at the view, while the car cooled. He had become a keen photographer and said, "I'll go back to the car and get the camera". He was a long time away. Mum went to investigate and found him slumped on the ground.

She started CPR. A passing couple stopped, one staying with Mum and the other went to stop someone for help. The first car had a nurse on board who took over the CPR until the Ambulance arrived and took them to the hospital where Dad was pronounced 'dead' and Mum was admitted.

Now it was my turn to act. I collected my sister, sixty-four kilometres away and drove the two hundred and forty kilometres to Dorrigo. When we arrived, the Matron said, "You have a remarkable mother. She is coping better than anyone I have ever seen under such circumstances". The reason was that she believed in God's power for protection. On the range, if the car had been moving, a much worse situation would have occurred. Dad was a Christian, so he was in Heaven, and Mum had God's comfort. I did the necessary identification and we did the long journey home with both vehicles.

Everyone can experience this truth in Matthew 5:4 "Blessed are those who mourn for they shall be comforted".

Reflection: Lord I thank you for all those moments when our grief seems to overwhelm us, and you send us comfort in many different ways.

Stop, You, don't need to go

Six vehicles in twelve hours! After my father-in-law's death, my mother-in-law and her sister continued to live in their Toowong home in Brisbane. My wife felt it would be good for them to come and spend a holiday with us in Bingara, New South Wales. I had to attend a professional meeting on Saturday night in Tenterfield, so we arranged for me to go on to Brisbane after the meeting and bring them both back the following day.

I left Bingara after lunch on Saturday and travelled the seventy kilometres to Inverell. Just as I reached town, my car stopped. I realized it was a repair job and stepped out on to the roadside. Along came a friend and took me to the Holden car sale yard. I knew the chief salesman and told him my urgent need of attending the meeting and picking up my mother-in-law and her sister in Brisbane. I asked, "Can I buy a car from you?" He was happy to do this and took care of the broken-down car.

This new car was two years old and had been passed in for the latest model. Also, the firm had fitted it with a new engine. I paid the cheque and left for the sixty-seven kilometre trip to Glen Innes. By the time I arrived, the engine was making a squeaky noise.

From a phone box, I rang the salesman, who assured me it would just be the new engine 'getting run in', to get in and continue on to Tenterfield. About twenty kilometres out of Glen Innes, the noise became much louder. I pulled off the road and began walking back to Glen Innes.

It was now getting dark, and along came a Land Rover Jeep with a dinghy and a lot of camping gear on top. He pulled up and said, "Do you belong to that new car up the road, and need a lift?" I gladly accepted. He said, "I don't often see a man in a suit walking along the road". He was one of the Leyland brothers returning from a documentary filming trip.

He let me off in Glen Innes and I rang the salesman again. He said "I'll come and bring the workshop foreman, and you'll soon be on your way." They arrived about an hour later and out to the new car we went. When the foreman heard the engine, he could see that it would have to be repair job. He towed it back to Glen Innes, where they left the car, and drove me back to Inverell. He loaned me a Utility to drive back to Bingara arriving home about 2 am.

First thing Sunday morning, my wife rang her mother to explain why I hadn't arrived in Brisbane to bring them down for their holiday. She said, "But we're not coming! Didn't you get the telegram?" That arrived two days later. It took six vehicles to stop me doing an unnecessary trip, and I was thankful.

The Good News Bible, in Proverbs 16:1 it says:" We may make our plans, but God has the last word."

Reflection: Father God, you work in so many mysterious ways that sometimes it is hard to comprehend them but I thank you that you do.

Another Fake

At Christmas time we enjoy the best food, the giving of gifts, and the celebrating the birth of the Christ Child, his life, death, and resurrection. Christ has made the greatest impact for good in the world. Even commerce has also taken up Christmas with great enthusiasm.

We have five children in our family and for each of them, their Birthday was their special day. By the time each one had a Birthday celebration and the remembering of Christ's Birthday at Christmas time, we had at least eight special days of giving gifts, special food, and a cake. The cake was the last in the day's function, together with the Birthday Song.

Often guests and friends would join in, creating quite a house full and making the day extra special for the one who was the centre of attention for the day. As the girls grew older, they wanted to out-do the boys, so the cake was given extra attention. On one occasion, one of the girls had a devious idea for the brother who played tricks on them.

They persuaded me to cut a suitable, cake size, block of wood, then raided mother's cupboard. With the cake plate under the block of wood, they let their artistic talents shine. The outcome was a most attractive cake as the centre piece of the table for the Birthday evening meal. When the time arrived for the cutting of the cake, the real content was not obvious until the son found that the knife would not penetrate this beautiful piece of art. He stopped in surprise, and with a questioning look at the imitation said, "This is a bit suss!" It was a beautiful fraud!

Bless her! Mother brought out the real thing and family trust was preserved. God's Word says in 1 Samuel 16:7b. "The Lord does not see as man sees; for man looks at the outward appearance, but the Lord looks at the heart."

Reflection: Father I thank you that you can always be trusted.

Easter Inspirations

The effects of Easter! When I remember the life, death, and resurrection of Jesus Christ, I realize He had made the world a better place.

Modern education was started by Christians giving children an opportunity to learn to read and write. They brought about freedom for slaves and made nursing a great profession. Most improvements to the world were begun by people who, because they believed in Jesus Christ as God's Son, wanted to express, by their work, His love for all.

Great buildings such as Cathedrals stand as tributes, while great paintings and music, as inspiration expressed in skill and harmony, lift our spirits to higher values.

The Bible tells of some of the reactions of personalities in the real-life happenings of that first Good Friday.

Pilate said, "I have found no fault in Him". Luke 23:14

Pilate's wife sent a message to her husband saying, "Have nothing to do with that just man, for I have suffered many things this day in a dream because of Him." Matthew 27:19.

The Centurion who was the Supervisor of the Crucifixion, expressed his fear and admiration after the earthquake and three hours of darkness, and said, "Truly this was the Son of God." Matthew 27:54

One thief on a cross next to Jesus, said, "Lord remember me when Thou comest into Thy Kingdom". Jesus said, "Today shalt thou be with me in Paradise". Luke 23:42-43.

Then, from my family's heritage, the Easter story became real to my Grandfather which brought to his descendants a quality of life they would not have had otherwise.

My Grandfather in 1888 always had work, even though he had an alcohol problem. One night, sitting by his campfire, he had a vision of Jesus on the cross, who seemed to be looking at him... Jesus, being crucified because He loved him, brought tears to his eyes.
Then on the 22nd December, 1888, he dreamed that he should get up and pray for what he wanted, and he prayed for forgiveness of his sins, and power to overcome his alcoholism. He said, "The glory of God filled my soul, I knew I was forgiven and that God loved me". He later became a family man and a productive citizen, retiring in his seventies.

Reflection: Father I thank you so much for the work of your spirit in the life of my great grandfather and for the many blessings that have flowed on down through the generations.

Deceived

Don't be deceived by first impressions.

1)   There is an incident which occurred in the Northern Hemisphere, on the property of a farmer who had a large ice block like object fall from the sky on to his paddock. He had never seen the like! Was it something from outer space? He removed a piece of it, stored it in his food freezer and called the Outer Space Research people. They came, showed great interest in it, and took the object away for examination. The farmer waited in great suspense for the results of this mysterious find. When it came, the Space Research Specialist told him that, without a doubt, it was the jettisoned contents from a high-flying aeroplane's toilet storage tank, the fluid freezing as it descended. Thus, the mysterious object had a logical explanation.

2)   Some years ago, I was watching TV with my young grandson, a 'goodies and baddies' film. Someone on the screen had been shot, the appropriate imitation blood was shown, and he was upset that the man was dead. When I tried to explain to him that it was "pretend, not real", he insisted it was real, saying, "No! Look at the blood!" I took his father aside and encouraged him to teach his son that much of TV was an illusion, and there is a difference between 'real' and 'false'.

3)   We lived in the warm parts of Queensland for some years before moving to a cold district in New South Wales. Our youngest daughter had never seen frost. When the cold came in with intensity, she went out on to the verandah early one morning in bare feet and saw the glistening white frost. She was delighted and before we could stop her, exclaiming "Pretty, Pretty, Pretty!" ran out on to the frost covered lawn. It immediately changed to "Ooh. Ooh, Ooh" and she made a hasty escape back to the warmth of the house. She learned there was more to "beauty" than glitter.

The first mysterious object carried undesirable content. The second, showed it is dangerous to build character on illusions. The third shows that some beauty can be deceiving.

The Bible says, "There is a way which seemeth right unto man but the end therefore are the ways of death." Also, in Galatians 6:7 "Do not be deceived, God is not mocked; for whatever a man sows, that he will also reap."

Reflection: Thank you Father for being able to show us the truth, please give us eyes to see and ears to hear even when that truth is uncomfortable for us to deal with.

Angels

One of my friends had a small, well run farm near an expanding coastal town. One day, a land developer came along and offered him a lot more money than he could get for it as a good farm, so he let it go for a housing project. He moved to town and his children were able to walk to school rather than having to catch a bus, but he was bored, so he found work in a factory. They soon gave him responsibility which he still found to be confining.

He bought a small block and it was not long until he had developed it to its capacity and felt he needed to do part time work to find fulfillment.

Then, someone introduced him to a widow who was distressed because the farm, which her husband had made successful, was being badly neglected. On the death of her husband, she had leased it to city people. They seemed to have had the idea that farmers were people who just milked the cows twice a day, and sat on the verandah while the rest just happened.

The widow said, "If you will buy this property and make it efficient again, I'll be so grateful." This started a trying time in his family's life. Things were much worse than they expected. Many of the cows were so neglected that he had to sell a lot of them. The irrigation had not been used and the river flats were overgrown with noxious weeds and the poultry had become feral. Hens, with chickens, would appear from under sheds. They caught many, but some were too wild to catch and had to be shot. The half kilometre drive from the road to the house became a water course in the wet.

When the agents noticed the irrigation working, hay being made, cows in larger numbers, fences repaired, driveway gravelled and buildings tidied up, they appeared in numbers hoping to sell their fertilizers, milking machines and fencing materials.

One morning, Bert had been up since 4 am and had unexpected troubles with his stock and was coming in for breakfast about 9 am. He was dirty, his rubber boots were muddy; and his hair in a dishevelled state, when up the drive drove another flash car. He said to his wife, "I'll go and meet this fellow and send him on his way." His wife said, "Bert, you can't go out in such a dirty state. You look like nothing on earth!"

His sense of humour came to the fore and out to the gate he went as the hopeful salesman was getting out of his car. He shook his hand, held it, and said, "Do I look like an angel?" The salesman's eyes widened, he looked a little confused and gave no answer. Bert calmed the poor fellow's startled reaction by saying, "My wife just told me I look like nothing on earth, so I thought I might look like an angel. We are not in the market for anything today and I need to have my breakfast." The relieved and puzzled salesman left in a hurry and Bert had his breakfast in peace.

The Bible tells us that there are real angels who care for us. In Psalm 91:11. "He (God) shall give His angels charge over you, to keep you in all your ways."

Reflection: Father, I pray that I will always be focused on you but please keep my feet earth bound so that I will not be so heavenly minded that I am of no earthly use.

Healing Hearts

Today, medical Specialists have changed the way to treat many heart conditions. Years ago, the treatment was mainly 'rest'.

We were living in a country town, and almost every day, an elderly gentleman would walk to the corner store, purchase two or three items, put them in his basket and walk back home. Then later, he would go back again and buy two or three more items and return home. This happened practically every day of the week, which was the way the groceries were bought. His wife did the yard jobs and the lawn mowing.

I enquired as to the reason why this elderly couple had made such arrangements for what appeared to be "role reversal" before it was recognized, of their chores.

"Oh", they said, "Years ago a Doctor told Mr.— that he was not to lift more than four pound or two Kilograms in weight, because of his heart condition. So, he walks to the shop, selects the weight in goods to comply with the doctor's orders, and his wife does the heavier jobs." This explained this different behaviour.

Another gentleman, in his young days, had been a stockman, when lassoes were used and the stock-whip was a 'must'. He became an expert with both. In retirement, he would go to youth groups and show how it was done in the past. He would get the young people to run in a circle while he stood in the centre. He was then able to lasso a leg as they ran past, as well as other precision feats with rope and stock-whip. He was in big demand to demonstrate these lost skills which we young people had never seen. His doctor told him that he would need to give up this activity, because his heart was not handling it very well.

He then decided to go to England for a holiday. This meant six weeks on the boat, spend six weeks in England and six weeks on the boat to return. Before he arrived in England, he fell and broke his leg. He was hospitalized for six weeks so his leg would heal. This meant no sight-seeing because it was then time to join the return voyage back to Australia. When he arrived home, he went to see his doctor, who asked, "What have you been doing?" He explained about his failed English trip. The Doctor replied, "That's the reason why your heart is so much better. You can go back to doing your rope and stock-whip demonstrations." That was when I knew of him.

There are conditions which modern medicines cannot heal; the happenings in life which break people's hearts, their spirits, or emotions. They need the touch of the Great Physician to have healing for these things. The Bible says "God heals the broken hearted and binds up their wounds." Psalm 147:3.

Reflection: I thank you with a grateful heart for all the times that you have allowed physical, emotional, and spiritual healing to take place in my life.

New Year and Eternity

In my visits to Sydney during my early years, I saw, written in chalk on the footpaths, the word 'Eternity'. In later years, it was also written on pieces of tin nailed to trees along the Highway into Sydney. Years after, the true story behind it came to public notice.

Arthur Stace was born in Balmain to an alcoholic father and a mother who ran a brothel. He was brought up in poverty, stole to eat and at twelve years of age was made a State Ward. He received no education and at fifteen years had his first jail sentence. He ran sly grog, drank plenty and acted as a 'cockatoo' (lookout) for gambling houses and brothels.

He served with the AIF as a stretcher bearer in France and returned home in 1919, suffering shell shock, damaged eyesight, and the effects of mustard gas poisoning. Back home, he soon slipped back into his old way of life; a petty criminal, a bum, and a Metho drinker.

In 1930 he went to a meeting for needy men. Among the three-hundred-odd there, he noticed a few well-dressed men standing near the door. He asked one of his mates, "Who are they?" referring to the well-dressed men. He replied, "I reckon they be Christians." To which Arthur replied, "Look at us and look at them! I'm having a go at what they've got."

After a cup of tea, something to eat and a Gospel message, he left the Hall; knelt under a Moreton Bay Fig Tree, prayed "God be merciful to me, a sinner", and God heard him. He said later, "I went for a cuppa and rock cake and met the 'Rock of Ages'. As I got back my self-respect, people were more decent to me." He was then able to find steady employment.

Two years later he went to hear an Australian Evangelist, John G Ridley MC, who at the end of his message emphasized the word ETERNITY. ETERNITY, I wish I could shout that word to everyone in the streets of Sydney. Where will you spend ETERNITY?

Arthur said, "I left with the word 'Eternity' on my brain and felt a powerful urge from God to write it. I had a piece of chalk in my pocket, so I bent down outside the Church and on the footpath, wrote 'eternity'. It came out in smooth copperplate script. I couldn't understand it then and I still don't. I'd had no schooling and I couldn't have spelled 'eternity' for a hundred quid.

From then on, this thin five-foot, three-inch man rose at 5 am every day and wrote in chalk, over the different Sydney footpaths, his one-word sermon. Twenty-four years later a minister saw him writing and said, "Arthur, are you Mr. Eternity?" His reply was "Guilty, your Honour." Mystery solved! Reports were then published in the papers and on TV and later a documentary was made of his life.

In the New Year Celebrations of 2000, for the entire world to see, Eternity was emblazoned in fireworks across the Sydney Harbour Bridge.

The Evangelist, J.G. Ridley had said he would like to tell it in every street in Sydney, yet a little man, with no theological training, never ordained, who could not read or spell, in God's plan, told the world.

Our best New Year's Resolution could be – Prepare for ETERNITY.

Reflection: I thank you, dear Lord, that, thanks to your son's sacrifice on the cross, those who believe in your grace get to spend eternity in Heaven.

Puppets

During the last few weeks, we have been sorting through our old records and papers, bringing back many memories.

Many were about the ways our children, needing to make their own fun and games, entertained themselves. This was before the magic box of TV. The stick horse was one way and this horse could perform all or even more feats than a real horse. The pet hen which was carried everywhere and was considered a boy's best friend, the tree house, built in the back yard where parents were only allowed to look on. The 'dress ups' which took the children to another world of make believe.

The old school reports reminded us of all the hours of homework that was put in with each of the children. For music lessons we had to travel 40 miles for a qualified teacher. The handmade cards for Christmas, Birthdays, and Mother's Days expressed real love in much more personal and real ways, as money was short.

Then we discovered a note written by my wife. It read: Saturday morning, after a week in which plumbers had been busy at work. Also, a washing machine break-down. Washing and ironing still had to done – Dad to get away to his job – when our 6-year-old asks "Mummy, can I make a puppet?" Oh dear! My first reaction was one of impatience, then the common side step of 'not enough time'. A wise and understanding father remarked, "You'll possibly need to help her, but it will probably be a good thing to do." With some reluctance, I agreed to try. An old Santa Claus head – part of a plastic nut and bolt set – some left-over red material- also part of her brother's worn out khaki shorts (kept for patching). I sat at the sewing machine, without changing the grey cotton, a red coat was made with a small opening, khaki hands stitched in and to my amazement, it was there in such a short time. The delight of the six- and three-year olds, the peace and contentment of playing happily with it for most of the day, was very rewarding. The fact that the opening was too small for the older children of the family was a decided advantage, making an exclusive toy for them, meaning less upsets. As I reviewed the sheer pleasure given to my two youngest by this simple puppet, I felt that the investment of those few minutes had paid tremendous dividends.

THOUGHT: May I keep my priorities right and not deny others the joy of some simple gift.

Reflection: I will always be grateful for the blessing of a mother who worked very hard at making sure that her priorities were right.

New Life

Have you finished all your Easter Eggs? They are a joy to children and an indulgence for chocolate lovers.

I remember a gentleman who had come from a city in Europe and had lived in Australian cities, where he had made his life very comfortable until he retired. He then travelled overseas for a tour of Europe and England and returned to settle in an Australian village for a tree change.

At first, it was a few chooks in the backyard, and then he decided to breed his own. When a hen went broody, he secured a setting of eggs and in three weeks, there were the chickens. He was amazed! His knowledge of eggs consisted of his wife putting them into cakes, cooking them in a pan or as scrambled eggs on toast.

For them to produce life in three weeks was so special that he kept bringing up the subject. His mind was stimulated to realize that in such a short time, yolk and white could become a new walking life.

In another State, a little country Church was surrounded by just a few houses. A traveling Minister conducted an Easter Sunday service, to celebrate Jesus Christ rising from the dead and coming out of the tomb.

A couple, with three children, whom he had not met previously, attended the service. The Minister showed an Easter Egg and asked the children, "What does this egg represent?" The answer he expected was "I'm not sure", or "An egg hunt", or "chocolate." The children answered in unison, "New Life".
"Who told you that?" asked the Minister.
"Mum and Dad. It represents Jesus' new life when He rose from the grave and is alive for ever". The Minister was pleased to see that there were still those who passed these Bible truths on to their children.

In the Bible, Romans 6:8-9, we read "Now if we died with Christ, we believe that we shall also live with Him, knowing that Christ, having been raised from the dead, dies no more. Death no longer has dominion over him."

Reflection: What a blessing it is to know that we can have a new life in Christ, simply because Jesus was able to rise from the grave on that first Easter Sunday.

Power of Prayer

If you drive into Inverell, N.S.W. about 66 kilometres west of Glen Innes, at the 60 kilometre per hour sign you will see large homes alongside an aerodrome for light aircraft. This was my Grandfather's farm at the turn of the twentieth century, where my father was born in a slab house. His father had grown a forty-acre crop of wheat; this was a large area for the early settlers in those days. There was no insurance for hail damage and settlers booked up their purchases at the local store until the crops came in and they were paid for their wheat.

Sam & Emily Morris

One summer's day, Grandfather could see a bad hailstorm coming in from the east. Years before, Grandfather had been freed from alcoholism by prayer and he believed in God's power and the power of prayer. He went to his room, knelt by his bed, and prayed, "God, I don't want the crop's money for myself, but to pay my account at the store. Protect our crop please." The storm came to the east boundary of the crop, moved to the north boundary, then back down the west boundary, leaving the crop unharmed.

The Bible says in Exodus 34:10, that God will do marvels. So for Grandfather, God did a marvel again.

Reflection: Oh Lord God, the way you work amazes me all the time. Thank you for being such a powerful God.

Saved

Norm and Saddler

Over the years I had a number of dogs, which are wonderful animals, giving unconditional loyalty even when we do not always appreciate their faithfulness. Now I know that I should have shown more kindness and understanding to them and should have praised them more. I cannot go back and do that, so I try to use my failures and shortcomings to improve my attitude to people for they are even more special in God's creation.

My first dog was a Pomeranian cross, called Saddler because of the white patch over his back. He had saved my cousin's life. As a toddler, my cousin had wandered to the creek, that was running strong after a storm up stream and he was being knocked over repeatedly. Saddler raced up to the house, barking in an excited and alarmed way, which brought my aunt to the rescue just in time to retrieve a waterlogged boy out of the current.

In our spiritual and emotional world, we are often knocked down, yet God said in Romans 10:13 "For whosoever shall call upon the name of the Lord shall be saved".

Reflection: What a marvellous thing you do, Lord, when you rescue us from drowning in our sins.

The Spark

When I visit museums and see the early model tractors which were our working machines in the war years, I am reminded of the good mechanics who kept them going with limited parts.

Kerosene Tractor – Photo courtesy Lyn & Laurie Campbell

On one occasion, when our Power Kerosene Tractor stopped, the magneto that supplied the spark had to be repaired. They don't use these old-fashioned things now. The tractor was in the paddock on the dirt. The mechanic dropped a very small screw, with no replacement available, how would he find it. He called for two, three-bushel potato bags. He collected all the dirt in the area where that screw could have dropped and put it on to one bag, then carefully sieved it through his hands onto the other bag. Eventually he came to the needed screw, put it back and the tractor came to life.

It reminds me that today so many people have all the parts to make a great life, but have lost one small element. They are depressed, unfulfilled, unmotivated. If just one small quality was added, then back would come the spark. FAITH, HOPE, or LOVE could put spark into their lives and make them DYNAMIC.

Reflection: It is a wonderful thing to see broken lives put back together by the power of your love and grace oh Lord.

A Good Servant

Wilfred Morris' bootmakers shop in Otho St Inverell

Some of the men who came into Dad's boot shop were often old men who had few to care for them. One old man struggled on a crutch, with the four fingers on one hand held together with a not too clean rag. He lived in one room connected to the old stables at the back of the pub. There were no conveniences, but it kept him dry. He said "I am full of arthritis from being wet and cold at night, from past times when I was a drover."

On Saturday mornings, my brother and I had to run the messages for Dad's business and paying the bills was one of those jobs. The rent was paid at the bank because they opened on Saturday mornings in those days.

One morning my brother was a little late getting back and the shop door was shut. He went around the back and let himself in. There was Dad, down on his knees, cutting the old man's hard and smelly toe-nails with his leather knife as there were no chiropodists in those days.

Jesus told His Disciples to wash one another's feet in John 13:14, He did not say anything about toe-nails. Our parents taught us by example to serve the needy.

Reflection: Thank you for the good examples of my parents, grandparents, and other Christians around me. Help me to honour them by being a good model to others.

Faithful to the End

The old Drover talked of the best days he ever had. The outback pubs often had a galvanized enclosure into which all the empty bottles were thrown. This enclosure looked like a hill of empty bottles in which rodents lived. In my travels, I have only ever seen one of these enclosures that was full.

In one of these, a good-looking sheep dog bitch had a litter of pups and they were feral. The Drover saw one pup that looked exceptional. To catch him he had to hide, so when the pup came out after some considerable time, he caught the distinctive young dog. This started a long training exercise. He used driving reins from his horse and cart, about ten metres long, to tether him. It took patience and kindness until the pup bonded with the drover. It was worth it. He was a wonder dog that worked sheep as if he had his master's mind and made droving a pleasure. The dog's loyalty was such that he was the envy of many other owners. The drover said, "All I had to do was put my saddle cloth down, and Wonder Dog would stay there until I returned, regardless of whether it was hours, days or nights later." Sadly, later this faithful dog was poisoned and died.

Years after, the old Drover said with great emotion "As I buried the greatest, most faithful dog I ever had, I took off my hat and said, "In honour of you, I will never drove another sheep." And I never did. From then on I stayed with cattle work."

Faithfulness is a quality we all need to practice. God says in Revelation 2:10 "Be thou faithful unto death and I will give you a Crown of Life."

Reflection: Lord, how good it is that the crown of life is available to all those who love you and serve you faithfully.

Bush Skills

The old drover, who came to Dad's boot shop, told stories of West and Central Australia. That country claimed many a beginner's life because of lack of water. It is easy to forget, that until European settlement, so much of the continent only had water in good seasons and then people and animals retreated to the permanent water until the next good time came.

Without roads and only a few tracks, you had to keep your directions right by keeping yourself at the correct angle to the sun (A skill I do not have).

A mirage, which is an optical atmospheric illusion due to the curvature of the light rays, is a trap for many greenhorns. You can see what appears to be an expanse of water, off in the distance. We have experienced these for ourselves, and if you changed your bearings, you were done. Only when the Resurrection happens will we know of the many unknown deaths caused by this phenomenon.

The drover said the most dramatic thing he'd ever seen on the edge of a mirage was an Afghan and his camel train with its supplies moving along but it appeared upside down. It would have had to have been over one hundred miles away.

With the use of his bush skills, he had ridden from Darwin to Adelaide on horseback at least once. In those days if you were droving cattle from Northern Australia to Adelaide, holding paddocks were very few. They drove the cattle by day and, as the cattle camped, they watched them from a distance at night, lest they became spooked and stampeded. One trip involved a particularly restless mob and as they came closer to Adelaide, they had, for the last fortnight, to be in the saddle day and night and that was where they had their only sleep. He said, "I never had been so tired, I thought I'd sleep for a week at least. You know our bodies are amazing, a night, a day and the next night sleeping and I was ready for the next outing."

The drover found in Australia, by experience, what the Poet said in Psalm 139:14, "I will praise Thee for I am fearfully and wonderfully made. Marvellous are Thy works and that my soul knoweth right well".

Reflection: Father I thank you that I am fearfully and wonderfully made by your gracious hand.

Salvation for a gambler

He was a slightly built man, a former jockey with a moustache stained brown with nicotine. How he arrived in town we never knew. He came to the boot shop looking lonely. Dad did something he did not do very often; he asked him if he was interested in God helping him in his life. To father's surprise, the man answered that he felt it was his only hope. He was a gambling addict and had lost his wife and son because of his addiction. He'd gone to put his last two shillings (twenty cents) on a horse. He got there too late and as he arrived, he heard the horse lose the race which meant that all he had was his two shillings. This is, of course, more than he would have had, had he got there on time to place his bet.

Dad explained what he needed to know for God to be able to help him. First, he needed to be aware of his sin, second, to believe that Jesus Christ paid for his sin on the Cross, and third, to thank God for forgiveness.

Mr. Newland and his Sulky

It took years for him to get established back into a productive life. One of the happenings, which some of his Church people found hard to understand, was that he'd tell them that he never remembered praying in a desperate race situation without winning. His great joy was riding back on the winner and loving the applause of the crowd. Now he realised how very fleeting all this was, since the Christian life now gave him lasting fulfilment.

Reflection: Thank you father that no one is outside the reach of your arm.

Sweating it Out

The jockey we spoke about in "Salvation for a Gambler" had some revealing stories to tell. On one occasion his brother had a very good horse which was running and winning some races. Some competitors wanted to put a stop to it. When he heard that his regular jockey had been asked to throw a race with their good horse for a consideration, he said to his brother, Sid, "You get ready to ride. I'll say to my regular jockey, 'I want you to pull the horse in the next race,' and because he feels guilty about it, he'll say 'No'. He'll tell those who wanted him pulled that it was going to happen and he will still get his pay and then our horse will have better odds. Then I want you to ride him to win and we'll put plenty on at the last minute."

The trouble was that Sid was a few pounds over-weight. Sid said, "How will I get the weight off?" "No trouble" said big brother. "I'll arrange it with the baker. When the bread is finished, we'll roll you up in lots of blankets and put you in the oven and you'll sweat it out." This they did. So, while Sid was in the oven, big brother goes to the Pub for a drink and forgot that Sid was sweating out lots of pounds.

Eventually big brother remembered where Sid was and there was a rush to see if he was still alive. As he was, they pulled him out, unwrapped him but of course he was barely able to stand. It was off to bed to be fed soup to give him strength to do the ride the next day. The horse and rider did win and the bets paid well.

Here is an extract from Hebrews 12:1-2 "....let us lay aside every weight, and the sin which doth so easily beset us, and let us run with patience the race that is set before us, looking unto Jesus the author and finisher of our faith........."

Reflection: I am so grateful that you Lord will not forget me.

Grandma's Wine

When my mother's mother died, leaving nine children, the youngest two were quite small. Their Grandmother came to take care of the household until matters were settled and some new routine was established. That was quite a difficult job, with grief to heal and emotions to settle.

With the older woman in charge of the house, the younger children, in particular, drew comparisons a lot of the time with the Mother they had just lost. Like most Grandmothers, she had a big heart and caring for the family was exhausting. At night when the littlies were settled, Grandma would bring out her flagon of wine and have a quiet glass.

The family's mother had been a strict teetotaller. In the eyes of the younger daughter, Grandma was wrong and she decided to put a stop to it. When the groceries arrived with the flagon, she tipped a portion out and replaced it with 'good old vinegar'. When Grandma came to have her 'night cap', she got into quite a state. Never had she had wine like this! So, in person she went to the store, demanded, and got a replacement bottle for this inferior wine which had been sold to her. Only years later was the true story told.

We often want to change people's lives because we think our way is the right way. Trying to do this can frequently mess things up, rather than help. God changes lives, gives quality of life, and His methods often surprise us.

In Isaiah 55:8-9 we read, "For My thoughts are not your thoughts, neither are your ways My ways, saith the Lord. For as the heavens are higher than the earth, so are My ways higher than your ways, and My thoughts than your thoughts."

Reflection: Lord I know that I must leave the teaching of others completely to you. I know that it will strengthen my faith when I wait for you to do it your way.

Someone Cares

My mother, in her later years, came and stayed in our home to escape the cold of the southern states. She was a good correspondent and finding a sunny spot, would write and answer the letters from her many friends. She could make scenery such as sunrise, sunset and garden so real in her letters, sharing God's creation in a way which made people feel important.

The phone rang one day and a stranger questioned me about my name. He asked, "Is your mother Elvie Morris?" When I said 'Yes', he asked to speak to her. After their conversation, I enquired about the caller, and she told me the story.

The caller had escaped lawful custody and had lived many years under another name. Becoming a Christian, he moved back to Queensland and gave himself up and had to finish his time in prison. Mother had written her interesting letters to him for years and now, on his release, she was the first person he contacted. We offered to have him come and meet mother but he declined. How important it is for us to know that someone cares. He had now moved back into society and mother went to Heaven in her 96th year, leaving many people feeling that someone cared through her letter writing.

The Bible, in 1 Peter 5:6-7, says "Humble yourselves therefore under the mighty hand of God, that He may exalt you in due time; casting all your care upon Him; for He careth for you."

Reflection: I thank you Lord again for the care that you give us each day.

Built on Rock Foundations

Castle Hill, Townsville QLD

With summer storms about, it brought to my mind some of the happenings in my wife's Grandfather's life. He had made his way to Australia from Norway at 15 years of age. He was a very resourceful and determined man, following the goldfields looking for the 'big find'. However, he became a builder to keep his family in stability. A number of their children were born in Charters Towers, but necessity required them to move to Townsville. They bought a block of land well up on Castle Hill, giving them a wonderful view. He built the home himself with extra strength to withstand the storms, and sure enough, in came a cyclone.

The neighbours further down the hill were watching and expecting his exposed house to be blown apart when their own roof was blown off, but Grandfather's house remained steady all through the cyclone.

When it comes to quality character building, Jesus told the story in Luke 6:47-49, "Anyone who comes to me and listens to My words and obeys them – I will show you what he is like. He is like a man who, in building his house, dug deep and laid the foundation on rock. The river flooded and hit the house but could not shake it, because it was well built. But anyone who hears My words and does not obey them is like a man who built his house without laying a foundation; when the flood hit that house, it fell at once – and what a terrible crash that was!"

Reflection: Help me Lord to stay in you and keep my feet on the rock of life, Jesus Christ.

Healing with the help of a Goat

Our first baby developed eczema as there was no milk to be bought in the outback mining town in the early days. Powdered milk was used for everything, including milk shakes which certainly weren't wonderful.

The rural villages had reasonable milking goat herds. They had developed these through the Department of Primary Industries supplying goat bucks of a milking strain (Shannon) and by destroying the feral bucks, the townspeople raised a reasonable strain of milking nannies for villagers who cared to milk a goat. We secured a nanny from Julia Creek, and we had her brought the three hundred and twenty kilometres in the dog box of the train. The 'dog box' was a compartment where the drovers' dogs were housed when a drover was a passenger. We gave the goat supplementary feed at home, and let her run during the day, when she joined other goats who did the school grounds over for extras, including papers. She would come home in the evenings.

Jean Morris and her goat

In this way we supplied the fresh milk needed, and the Eczema cleared up on our toddler. As good milk helped to bring good health to our child, Jesus talks about spiritual sickness in the Gospel of Mark 2:17 .... "They that are whole have no need of the physician, but they that are sick: I came not to call the righteous, but sinners to repentance."

Reflection: I am always amazed at all the different ways you bring about the physical and spiritual health of those who trust in you.

Homemade Remedies and Prayer

Before the Second World War, our family lived in town and enjoyed its conveniences which were not available to our country relatives. They often came to my parents' home when they were in town on business. One of their men had developed peritonitis, was seriously ill and had been admitted to hospital. I looked up an old medical book and the explanation was in one short sentence which read 'Peritonitis is a serious illness and is frequently fatal.'

I remember a number of distressed aunts arriving at our home. The eldest of them said "My mother believed in Bran Poultices." She had asked the doctor if she could use them on the uncle. The doctor said, "Yes, I have done all I can, you're free to try." Our home was near the hospital, so they came to use our kitchen to make the poultices. I was sent to the shed with a large baking dish to fill with bran, which was heated in the oven of our wood stove. The poultices were made, and the ladies carried them backwards and forwards to the hospital.

They prayed for God to heal through the medical care, together with the old mother's remedy and the uncle recovered and returned to his farm.

1 Peter 3:12 reads: "For the eyes of the Lord are upon the righteous, and His ears attend to their prayer, but the face of the Lord is against those who do evil."

Reflection: It is such a blessing to know that you can use all sorts of people to carry out your plans, both small and large.

Signs to Follow

When my mother's people shifted to North West N.S.W. to settle and work the land, they started with many challenges. These included the putting together of structures, such as building housing and sheds, yards, and dams. They had to deal with drought, flood, and fire, all those things which make Australians unique. In those days, it was all done without the assistance of the improved equipment that we have today. It required them to use their own resourcefulness and staying power.

For education, their three oldest daughters had to attend a one-teacher school some four miles away, as the crow flies. This meant travelling on horseback or walking through the largest station where cattle ran unsupervised.

Grandfather walked the most direct route and cut the bark off the white Box trees close enough so the girls could follow them as they walked alone the four miles to and from school each day. The signs on the trees were for their safety. Two of the three girls went on to become school teachers themselves.

We can become successful in life by following God's sign posts and walking in the ways He has provided.

Proverbs 2:6 tells us "For the Lord giveth wisdom: out of His mouth cometh knowledge and understanding."

Reflection: Lord, help me to look for the signs of your love and care in the most ordinary situations in life.

A Destroyed Piano

Down the creek from our farm was one of the best examples of the old-time slab houses which early settlers lived in. The bark roof had been replaced with galvanised iron, but inside, the walls were still covered with newspaper to keep out the draughts. Their conveniences consisted of a wood stove and kerosene lamps.

The last couple who ran this farm seemed to have always been there. No one could remember when they had come. They worked with the minimum of necessities and no modern conveniences.

Neighbours regularly looked in to make sure they were all right. On one visit they found a new piano gracing the news papered wall. The couple had come into some money but No! They did not want conveniences. The lady bought a piano because that was a culture article, even though she could not play the beautiful thing and had no idea how to look after it. When neighbours called some months later, the keys were all warped and lifting. They asked what had happened to the piano. She said, "The bugs had got into the felt, so I killed them by pouring a kettle of boiling water over the keys." The beautiful piece of culture was unable to produce any music because of her bad decision. If someone had explained that ivory keys are destroyed by boiling water, the musical instrument would have been saved.

The Bible tells us in Proverbs 9:9. "Give instruction to a wise man, and he will be still wiser; Teach a just man, and he will increase in learning."

Reflection: Father, help me to learn even the smallest lessons that you bring to my attention.

Penicillin

Over the years, I have had some very talented musicians who provided accompaniment in our Church worship. In one town, the owner of an electrical and musical business was our musical director. He was a master of any organ, keyboards, or brass instruments. Playing the Last Post and Reveille on Anzac Day or on any other occasion, he performed with pleasure.

We were fortunate to have him at all, because he had been a dispatch rider in the military and had had an accident while on duty. He was examined by a doctor who decided there were no broken bones and concluded he would be able to resume duties. After some days, however, his pain increased and he became quite ill. It took some time for the medicos to make a serious investigation. They decided that the doctors should operate on him hoping to find the cause of his condition. When they opened him up, they found one kidney badly damaged and quite a number of organs had become gangrenous from an infection.

What could they possibly do? They said that there was a new substance, which was supposed to work wonders and they could try it on him as they didn't even expect him to live. This is what they told him later. They cleaned up the infection as best they could and took away the offending kidney.

He became one of the first people to be treated with Penicillin, and to the amazement of the doctor, he recovered. When we knew him, he was a happy, energetic family man, a prominent business proprietor, an active citizen in the town and the Musical Director of our Church.

He particularly appreciated the following verses of Psalm 23:4- "Yea, though I walk through the valley of the shadow of death, I will fear no evil; for You are with me; Your rod and Your staff, they comfort me." And especially verse 6: "Surely goodness and mercy shall follow me all the days of my life."

Reflection: Sometimes the blessings that you send us, oh Lord, come in very different forms, help us to see them for what they are.

What happened to...

Coonabarabran, a country town in North Eastern New South Wales, was situated in one of our Church areas, but was a long way from the centre. It was only possible to conduct a Service there once a month. When we also visited in the district and learned something of the town's past history, we discovered that, before the First World War, my wife's father started his trade there as a baker, working for his brother who ran a bakery business in town.

It was from Coonabarabran that he enlisted for his war service and his name is listed on their War Memorial. Our children and grandchildren are encouraged to visit the monument to make them aware of the price which was paid for our freedom.

One day, while visiting in the residential part of the town, I met a senior lady, who said, "I remember a young man who worshipped in your Denomination. I was sweet on him, but he went away to the First World War and I have never heard of him again. We all had to make our own lives after the war. I married and lived locally. "The young man's name was Bob Deans. Have you ever heard that name?"

I was able to tell her that I married his youngest daughter, that Bob had been wounded in France and had spent a long-time rehabilitating, not only physically, but also emotionally and had nerve problems. He was well into middle life before he married, and had a son and two daughters. This encouraged the exchange of happenings over all those intervening years.

What continually surprises me is the wonder of the spirit of mankind which God has placed in each person, wanting the best for those we have loved and the lasting memories of those days past which bring joy and light to the eyes and a smile to the face. Some experiences of the past bring pain and stress, yet love and caring bring healing and understanding for others.

In Luke 4:18 Jesus said, "The Spirit of the Lord is upon me, because He hath anointed me to preach the gospel to the poor; he hath sent me to heal the broken-hearted, to preach deliverance to the captives, and recovery of sight to the blind, to set at Liberty them that are bruised."

Reflection: Lord, I am continually amazed at how you move things into place in order to have your plans work, Lord, it just amazes me!

Bundaberg Anzac Padre Hero

William McKenzie (1869-1947), by unknown photographer, 1918
Australian War Memorial, P00329.001 [detail]

A Bundaberg boy was brought up in regular Church worship and instruction, but he often got into fights at school. The last fight, before he left school at thirteen years of age, was never really settled. One day he saw his previous enemy approaching and readied himself for another fight. However, the other boy approached with an extended hand and said, "I'm glad to see you, I want to tell you that I have been converted to the Lord Jesus Christ and it is wonderful." Astonished and a little shame-faced, the Bundaberg boy took the proffered hand and was mystified, as experiential knowledge of God's power through Jesus Christ had not come to him through his religious education.

Years went by and in his late teens he was given responsibility in his work, but his questioning was always, "Is there a God and a life hereafter?" He was awakened one night by a voice saying, "Go into Bundaberg to an Evangelistic Church." This was repeated for three nights, so on the weekend, he rode his horse sixteen miles into town. He was late, the Service being nearly over and the Preacher was asking those seeking God to come forward. He did this, and knelt at the front.

The first counsellor was not very clear. He promised him a wonderful thrill as though an angel somehow would put a great chunk of joy into his heart. He waited for that angel. Someone wiser came and said, "It is a contract." He understood that "God does His part and you are to do yours." He quoted the Bible, Jesus said, "Him that comes to Me I will in no wise cast out". I came to God in my need, believing He was the only One who could meet my need and that He was able and ready to do so. I said "I will trust God to save me now and with the prayer, 'God be merciful to me, a sinner' he rose from his knees, forgiven. He had lots to learn, but worked at it with the same vigour he had used in his school day fights.

As his knowledge of God's workings grew, he went to Melbourne to train as a full time Minister of the Gospel. When he qualified, he had a number of churches, but when the First World War broke out, he became a Padre and served at Gallipoli. He wrote of the costly assault of Lone Pine: 'The sight was awe-inspiring to see the first 2,000 odd jump out of the trenches and dash across the open in the face of intense shell fire, machine, gun and rifle fire. They were irresistible, performing marvellous feats.... The price was a heavy one... I was there in it all... The trenches were the most awful sight I have ever witnessed. Hundreds of dead; tiers deep in some trenches, the dead lying on top of the wounded.... And what a terrible struggle to get the wounded out! All night long we laboured, the stretcher-bearers performing heroic deeds under galling fire.'

On this occasion he toiled with wounded and dead for three days and nights without rest, and with only three biscuits and six pannikins of tea for nourishment, burying in that period no fewer than 647 men. By the end of that time he was so exhausted by lack of rest and food, and so torn with the sight of suffering and the loss of so many he knew, that, he confessed afterwards, he wished inexpressibly for death.

On an occasion when Colonel Unsworth was holding a meeting in one of the largest hospitals in Cairo, "In the midst of his address he mentioned Padre McKenzie. A poor man, badly wounded, struggled to raise himself and in a thin voice cried: 'Boys, a cheer for dear old Mac'. Colonel Unsworth recalls, "Oh, how those men did cheer! What a name "dear old Mac" had made for himself in the Dardanelles. The men tell such strange stories of his heroism. I scarcely dare relate half of them. But these brave fellows love him with a strange, wonderful love. I have not seen anything like it before, and proud must be the man who has made such a conquest. They speak much of his nerve but more of his real religion, of his prayer meetings with them when death was near. Their fear for his safety was so great that again and again they interposed their own bodies between him and the threatening shrapnel. Often too, they begged him not to expose himself to danger. 'Boys' he said to them once, 'I've preached to you and I've prayed with you, and do you think I'm afraid to die with you.'.

This man was William McKenzie MC.OBE.OF. of the Salvation Army. You can read more in the book 'William McKenzie, Anzac Padre'. The Church should note that it's not rules, regulations, rituals, and ceremonies that give power to Christian people, but faith in Jesus Christ, living as He did with love and care.

It is interesting to note that when William McKenzie came back to Australia, there was held a Welcome Meeting in Melbourne Exhibition Building at which it was estimated that 6,000 attended and hundreds were turned away.

Reflection: Thank you for the complete changes you can bring to our lives when we trust in you.

Leather Shoes

Today we buy footwear, shoes, boots, and joggers, wear them, and when worn out, throw them away. Not many people remember there was a time when there was no plastic and less rubber. Most of the footwear was made of leather.

My father was a bootmaker by trade and all the variety of leathers he used were stored in different sections of his shop. The soft leathers were for the uppers of shoes, the best and most flexible was made from kangaroo hide and used for the best ladies' shoes, called 'Pumps'. These were turned inside out, hand sown to the sole with a handmade thread waxed with Cobbler's wax to preserve it. The shoe was held between the knees while the bookmaker sat on a low stool. The holes were made with a hand awl, then a flexible like needle (I've forgotten its name) was used to pull the handmade thread through. When the sole was completely sown on, the shoe was turned the right way out and the ladies had an up-market shoe, which did not reveal the way it was held together.

There was also the straight forward sole and heel work for most school, business and walking shoes, held on by tacks. There were different grades of leather for these. The best, heavy working boots, called hob-nailed, had specific nails and horse-shoe like caps on the heels. Leathers for these were made from fully matured bullock or cow hides. They came in what they called bends of leather', the whole hide having been cured. The brands could be seen, indicating the station of owners of the cattle. Dad knew some of the stations and their owners.

As the years progressed, some leathers showed little pin marks all over them. It was then that my father realized that ticks had become a problem in the Queensland cattle country. The parasite left marks there forever. It is a fact that the marks of life, whether good or bad also are left on us forever. However, we can be useful and successful whatever the start we have, for we are all special, with different capacities.

The Bible says in Philippians 4:13, "I can do all things through Christ who strengthens me".

Reflection: Father, I thank you that, just like the shoes, we all have very different jobs to do for you that are related to the talents you have given us.

My Town

Inverell Railway Station – Photo courtesy of Inverell Times

I grew up in a country town which was situated at the end of the railway line. The town is called Inverell. All the goods which were not produced locally came by train. Carriers and those to collect passengers were there to meet the train and take them to their destinations.

Commercial travellers came by this means of travel, carrying two large ports each, in which were their samples of the goods from the firms they represented. They would spend the number of days in town necessary for getting orders from the businesses and then return by train.

The train carried all the goods which were exported from the town, livestock and farm produce, as well as the locally manufactured goods. The town had its own butter and bacon factory, flour mill, brick works, sawmill, and soap factory. The butchers killed their own meat at their killing yards. Most vegetables were grown in the district, according to the season, and bakers used flour from the local mill. There were a number of different blacksmiths and wheelwrights. There was a public hospital, three private hospitals and two locally owned newspapers. The town was one of the first to have its own electric power station.

When modern conveniences like motor vehicles came, there were bus runs and taxis. Some enterprising men started a radio station and a picture theatre. All sports clubs had their own committees. There was also a Pipe Band and three Brass Bands.

A three-day Show brought the people together annually, where they displayed their skills, wares, and stock. Competition was intense, the side shows were a way of showing the resourcefulness of those who made a living by entertaining and moving on from one place to another.

The streets of the town were the responsibility of a Street Cleaner, who used a push cart, shovel and broom to remove horse manure and rubbish. There were fewer rules and regulations, but people and firms succeeded by their efficiency and quality of article. This was demonstrated by the four department stores. Business owners were responsible for the footpath in front of their shops.

There were no dog registrations, so there were plenty of dogs running free in the streets. The dogs have a way of marking their presence by cocking their leg and wetting the corners of the stores and the awning posts. In the mornings, the people allocated the job of sweeping the footpath, could be seen with a bucket of water, washing off the doggy marks.

One store, with large corner frontage, solved the dog problem by building neat little water troughs for the dogs to drink from, at all the corners and doorways of their store. These were filled with fresh water daily. No dog wants to contaminate his drinking water, which solved their cleaning problem, as all the dogs drank from these corner troughs and moved further down the street to relieve themselves elsewhere.

Water is necessary to life for both animals and people. It satisfies the physical and also the spiritual, as the Bible says in St. John 4:13-

14. Jesus said, "Whoever drinks of this water (well water) will thirst again, but whoever drinks of the water that I shall give him will never thirst".

Reflection: I thank you for the history that surrounds the town of my birth. May we always be grateful for the blessings that you have bestowed on us.

Christmas changes the World

"For unto us a child is born, unto us a Son is given; and the government will be upon His shoulder. And His Name will be called Wonderful Counsellor, Mighty God, Everlasting Father, Prince of Peace." Isaiah 9:6.

Jesus was born in a manger, grew up and worked as a carpenter, never wrote a book, never owned property, borrowed the boats in which He sailed, and the donkey on which He rode into Jerusalem was owned by someone else. He cared for the poor, healed the sick, comforted the sorrowing and went about doing good, and our calendar dates are measured by His life (BC and AD). Many of the organizations which are now doing good, making life better for the recipients and fulfillment for those working in them, commenced from a love for Jesus Christ – born in a manger.

William Wilberforce, after he became devoted to Jesus Christ, the Baby born in a manger, gave liberally to schools for the poor, unemployed and destitute and planned to donate a quarter of his large income to help the needy. British Prime Minister William Pitt asked him to lead the fight against the Slave Trade in the British Empire. He spent the rest of his life (46 years) working in that capacity. On his death bed he received the news that the House of Commons had passed the Bill for the abolition of the Slave Trade.

Elizabeth Fry wanted to show the love of God, Whose Son was born in a manger. She visited the Women's Prison where over three hundred women and children were crowded together. They had poor bedding, food, and water, and they washed and dressed together. She spent her life changing the prison system to places where there were opportunities for reform for those who wanted to change.

Florence Nightingale's great life achievement was lifting 'nursing' from an undesirable job to a dignified profession. Her inspired motivation was of the great Healer, Jesus who was born in a manger.

Dr. Barnardo's Homes were started in 1867 to provide shelter and education for children who were hungry, homeless, and alone. Because this need still exists, these homes are still operating today. Dr. Barnardo made this his life work because he followed the Helper of the needy, Jesus Christ, born in a manger.

The Red Cross was commenced by Henri Dunant putting his personal wealth into getting it established. He became a caring man because of the influence of the Baby born in a manger.

We wish you all a very happy Christmas and may you be a blessing to others.

Reflection: Thank you for all your servants who have faithfully served throughout history. May we not forget the sacrifices that they have made and strive to do the same in your name?

Pioneers

The last of the early settlers, which I knew when they were old men, had years before opened up the farming district around Inverell. If only I had learned more from them, I would be wiser today. How different they were!

One, Paddy Davis, was the town saddler and harness maker. I remember him sitting in a squatter's chair on the foot path in front of his shop. As a lad, I was in awe of him, but I loved the smell of leather and Neat's Foot oil. In a gruff voice, he would say, "I'm going to live 'till I'm 100." He had earlier developed a block out of town with water and good fencing. By that time, he was too old to run stock on it.

The next property to his was owned by two bachelor brothers who lived in a one room slab hut, which they built while they were carving the farm out of the bush. They both suffered from asthma, were past working, and so had stock on agistment on their property. We mustered the cattle there into stock yards where even the gates were made entirely of round timber. They turned on the bottom of bottles that were upside down in the ground. When we called into to see them and report on the condition of the stock, they would be sitting on the steel stretcher beds under which were stacked many years of newspapers. My impression was that they were so old and sick. They finally had to sell up and leave what they had lived and worked for all their lives. Their machinery sale was like an antique sale which brought people from all around the district to see what the living in the early days was like.

The next property was called 'Bramble Tor' (Welsh for prominent hill). The owner, Mr. Landers lived in town in a big home on a hill with a long drive and grounds. He went to check his workers and property in his car. (Few people had cars).

I now realize that the people who made our country great were very different people in their values and the way in which they made their properties productive. Will the people, who now live on these farms in new homes with every convenience give any thought to the long-term care of the part of the Planet they live on and for which they are now responsible?

Proverbs 22:2-3a reads, "The rich and poor are alike before the Lord who made them all. A prudent man foresees the difficulties ahead and prepares for them;"

Reflection: Father, help us all to remember the wisdom of those who have cared for both our land and country and give them the honour that they deserve.

The Cross of Peace

My Grandfather started work, at 11 years of age, in a factory in London. When he was 15, his parents left London, and he had to make his own way. His work was among men, some of whom declared that there was nothing beyond this life, and others said they were Christians, but their lives proved the opposite. He took to the strong drink and by 17 he had become a drunkard. The men he worked with warned him that he would die in the ditch if he didn't pull up. He wandered around England, doing things when drunk, which could easily have killed him. Finally, his father paid for his passage to Australia. He told his pals that he was going to Australia for a change of air and spent his last shilling on beer before he boarded the boat.

Australia, being a large country, gave him plenty of area to roam, and he, being a blacksmith, plenty of work, money, and drink. This resulted in an accident when he was drunk which almost killed him. This made him realize that it would be 'drink and die' or 'get help.'

By his camp fire, one night, he saw in the flames, a vision of Jesus Christ on the Cross, looking straight at him. This brought tears to his eyes and he promised to love and serve God. On December 22nd 1888, he prayed, asking God to forgive his sin, and to help him in the future.

He then lived a very fulfilling life until his death in 1930. Here is a Padre's story to remember:

He knelt beside a young soldier who was dying and was not at peace. The Padre had an inspiration to make a cross of two sticks, tied them together and gave them to the soldier. As he held it, his facial expression changed, and while the Padre prayed, the boy's spirit left him. It was the Cross which gave him peace. Good Friday is a 'Good Day'. Remember what gives us peace with God and ourselves.

Reflection: For the peace that you give us that we can never understand, I thank you, Lord.

Mission Settlements

After the war, as I travelled by boat down the west coast of Cape York Peninsular. The boat called in to the Mission Settlement of Mapoon. We had by-passed the Weipa Mission by crossing Albatross Bay, (they were still to become aware of the great bauxite deposits there) and then on down to Aurukun. These were three missions run by the Presbyterian Church. Further down the coast there were the Edward River and Mitchell River Settlements, run by the Church of England.

Missions have sometimes been criticised by people who knew little about the conditions under which people there lived and worked. I think the missionaries were some of the most remarkable people I have ever met.

Rev. McKenzie and his wife had then been at Aurukun for twenty-five years, and when our boat came in, they had not received any mail for six months. They eagerly read the old letters and magazines with intense interest! This isolation was a major part of the lives of the people living there in those times. With our modern communication, it is hard for us to appreciate their situation.

After the First World War, the McKenzie's started to build the village by clearing the bush. The houses were built high so that native fires for outdoor cooking could be done underneath. In the wet season they went upstairs to live in dry conditions. Numbers of the natives still lived most of their lives in the bush, only coming in for emergencies and when food was scarce.

The commitment and care given to the natives by these Missionaries was excellent. The job of introducing these people to the modern world in a twenty-five-year time span makes one's mind boggle.

Father Brown at Edward River lived alone with the tribe which he taught to build Pandanus Palm huts to live in. What courage he had and how the natives respected him. These men and women must have remembered the promise of Jesus in Matthew Chapter 28:20 "...Lo, I am with you always, even unto the end of the world."

Reflection: For the courage of those who have gone before us in your strength, Father help us to use your strength to follow where you lead us.

Fishing at Sea

I was an inland boy who had only fished with a bent pin for carp and only ever visited the sea three times.

What I saw from a sailing boat down the West coast of Cape York (there was no commercial fishing there in those days), really opened by mind to another world of marine life. Seeing a shark swallow a meat tin thrown overboard, with the ease that I swallow a tablet, amazed me. For a change from the tinned food, the native boys robbed a turtle's nest and boiled the eggs, the yolk goes hard and the white remains clear and soft. It was certainly a change!

I had never seen or even heard of Dugong (Sea Cow) till I saw one landed for a tribal feast. What a party!

Fishing from a boat in the Archer River was done with heavy window cord and a hook the size of which I had never seen before, and a red rag for bait. They caught a large fish; put the boat oar through its mouth and out its gill to stop it jumping out of the boat. It was cut up like a sheep and the chops were lovely.

I kept my mouth shut to protect my ignorance. I was learning new things every day. These real experiences could have gone forever, leaving only stories to tell, which people find hard to believe.

They show the Bible's truth of God's creation and man's power over it, as the Bible records in Psalm 8:8-9 "...The fowl of the air, and the fish of the sea, and whatsoever passeth through the paths of the seas. O Lord our Lord, how excellent is Thy Name in all the earth."

Reflection: For the different ways of learning, Lord, we thank you.

No Boomerangs

The Missionaries had encouraged the natives to retain their 'bush gathering and hunting skills'. They therefore kept their ability to make their own equipment, woven carry bags, fire sticks (a fire could be started as quickly with these as with matches), spears for different uses, and woomeras to give greater power and distance when throwing a spear.

There were no boomerangs on Cape York. When I asked the makers of their equipment about the absence of boomerangs, they gave me a look as if I was lacking in observation. When I pressed for an answer, they said "We do not make them and do not know how to use them, for here the Boomerang is useless. There are too many trees, this is forest country only. Tribes who live on the plains or lightly timbered country use Boomerangs. You cannot throw them through trees."

Many of the natives I met had multi-skilled capabilities, having acquired European work experience, and yet retained their native abilities. One native Christian couple lived and travelled with the bush people, sharing with them their Bible knowledge, praying with and for them, teaching them that God hears, no matter where they are.

Jeremiah Chapter 33:3 says "Call unto Me, and I will answer thee, and shew thee great and mighty things that thou knowest not."

Reflection: For your faithfulness to us, we thank you.

Sunday Lunch in the Outback

In a dry season, at Mitchell River on Cape York Peninsular, motor vehicle traveling could be done overland quite satisfactorily. While I was there, the folk visited the neighbouring station, Rutland Plains, for a Sunday lunch. We followed a track through the bush, crossed various water courses which were dry enough not to cause delays and enjoyed the neighbours' wonderful bush hospitality.

Shortly after we arrived, two horsemen rode in. They had the fine physical appearance of which the outback people are very proud. They had ridden for hours from an outstation on Dunbar Station, as Sunday was a 'rest day' for them. A great time was had by all – plenty of good food and the kind of conversation which cattlemen enjoy.

It came time to return and the horsemen were the first to leave, for they had hours to ride through the bush, we were the next, only we had tracks to follow. As the horsemen rode off, the Manager of Rutland Plains said, "The head horseman there, he's a dentist by profession. Why he is almost as far away as possible from the civilized world and his technical practice, we don't know. In these parts you don't ask questions about one's past, just accept and enjoy what each has to offer."

My mind, even after all these years, has asked, "Why would a Doctor of Dentistry be as far away as possible, making him feel the need of isolation?" That secret is none of my business. When we feel a broken spirit or loneliness, I believe the answer is, not isolation, but to seek real help.

God said, "He shall call upon Me and I will answer him: I will be with him in trouble; I will deliver him and honour him." Psalm 91:15.

Reflection: Thank you for loving us with all our faults and secrets, Lord.

Scurvy

Mitchell River Mission was well established. It had street lighting, a store, a butchery and fruit and vegetable gardens as well as being a working cattle station. In Normanton, there was a family who had committed their lives to working with the Aboriginal people there. For them life was hard with little financial support. During the dry season they could not have a productive garden and fresh food was scarce.

The message brought by the natives who came to Mitchell River, was that the children of this family were showing signs of ill health. As I had planned to visit Normanton, the Mitchell River Manager said, "We will make up a parcel of fresh meat and vegetables, because by the description I'm getting, I think the children are showing signs of Scurvy, and the fresh food would help them."

In history, at school, I had learned about Scurvy as an early day sailor's complaint, but even in those days I thought it was no longer a problem. However, when I arrived, sure enough, the children had sores and scabs around their mouths. In the short time I was there, the fresh food made a visible improvement in their condition. We are blessed now with refrigeration and health services which make for an improved way of life.

In neglect of our spiritual and emotional world, we too can become unhealthy in the inner person. Therefore, we need to feed our spiritual being with the qualities of love as outlined in 1 Corinthians 13 which emphasizes kindness, lack of envy, not being easily made angry, being truthful, having faith, hope, and love.

Reflection: For your word that enables us to gain fresh spiritual insights every day, I thank you, oh Lord.

Under Steam Power

On my first visit to Cloncurry, I was young and needed to move on but a few years later I was to spend some time in that town. The first train out was a goods train with a carriage for wanderers like myself.

Steam power was wonderful, but there was no hurry. Someone suggested the theme song "I'll walk beside you." They stopped and waited at all the sidings. The crew stopped for 'smoko' and meal breaks, getting their hot water from the engine, but passengers could only get theirs at some of the stations.

When it was time to move on, the whistle blew, but there was no rush, just a stroll to the track side where they waited until the carriage came along side, then the engine paused and we climbed aboard and moved to the next stop. Fettlers camped by the line for a week at a time and received their provisions by train. This trip made slower time than the sailing ship down Cape York Peninsular. Townsville was a long way away at that pace.

The first night I learned how cold the inland plains could become. My father had talked about men who had used newspaper for warmth, so the next day I made it my business to collect a few newspapers at various stops, the dates did not matter. The next night I used them to good effect. The other travellers with me were more experienced and seasoned men and their yarns made the slow traveling time quite educational. When we eventually reached Townsville, my first stop was for a good meal. When we passed through Julia Creek, I got a cup of tea and the paper but took very little notice of my surroundings. Little did I realise that years later, I would spend days there waiting for a flood to go down.

The future is known to God, and we are assured in Proverbs 3:6 – "In all thy ways acknowledge Him and He shall direct thy paths."

In hind-sight I have had a very interesting life and am glad I have let God be my guide.

Reflection: Lord, help us to remember that you do not require us to rush around but sometimes you want us to take life at a slower pace.

Sails to Steam

The sailing boat which recently beached on the East Coast reminded me of my first trip to Sydney. We travelled by steam train from North West New South Wales to Newcastle, during the 1930's with a stop there to see the steel works and a multi-storey hospital where my aunt was doing her maternity training. They all looked so big.

We then continued on to Sydney by steamboat. The men occupied the fore-cabins and endured the roughest travelling while the ladies and young children were at the aft. This was where my mother and young brother travelled while Dad and I were up the front with the men, who were mainly commercial travellers with their large ports containing samples of the goods sold by their firms.

It was an overnight trip, coming through the Sydney Heads early in the morning. Dad took me up on deck to see ocean going sailing ships moored with their sails all folded up and looking very majestic.

Dad said, "Son, take a good look at those sailing ships for you might never see them like that again." He knew that steam was doing away with sailing ships for cargo transport. I remember looking carefully at that scene, trying to imprint that picture in my mind.

Isn't the mind wonderful! For I can still recall that picture even after all these years. Dad followed the Bible principle in Deuteronomy 4:9; "Only take heed to yourself, and diligently keep yourself, lest you forget the things your eyes have seen, and lest they depart from your heart all the days of your life. And teach them to your children and your grandchildren." This same method of teaching was used in our family for matters like honesty, kindness, manners, and faith in Jesus Christ.

Reflection: I thank you that you are always a faithful God.

A Bird's Profanity

In horse and coach days, the resourceful pioneers established centres where their horses could be changed every twenty miles and travellers could rest and have a meal.

When the railway came into privileged areas, the distance between towns became about one hundred kilometres. Barracks were provided for drivers and staff. Maintenance men and fettlers lived in homes with their families and camped along the track during the working week. On my trips, I would visit the towns which had sprung up along the railway line.

At one town, on the first morning, I was awakened by a screeching voice using the largest vocabulary of swearwords and profanity I had ever heard put together. As it did not sound altogether human, I assumed it must have been a talking bird greeting the wonders of a new morning in its acquired communicating skills.

During the day, I met the lady who was the caretaker of this remarkable bird. She hurriedly apologised for the bird's language, thinking that it would have offended a clergyman. I believe if you can swear in front of God, don't worry about the Parson.

She explained that the bird had been rescued by a team of fettlers and had been taken in a cage with them each week on their camps. It had sat in the dark and listened to the campfire conversations with their adjectives, and in this way had learned these words and phrases which it screeched out each morning.

If the bird learned this so well, how careful we should be about what our children hear from us, because this will mould their behaviour for the future.

Proverbs 22:6 says "Train up a child in the way he should go, and when he is old, he will not depart from it."

Reflection: How good is it that you teach us, your children, good things, oh Lord, even if the lessons are hard.

The Headstone

I was following a new bulldozed track. Where would it take me? There was no sign or trace of bygone days' activities. The dozer had followed the water course which was now dry, then gone up a stony ridge.

There on the side, obviously left by the dozer driver out of respect, stood a small marble head-stone. On it was the name of a child, its age in months, dated before 1910. I have forgotten the exact year, for my mind was living the parents' experience of those struggling years. When the family was following the water course, the baby had died. They had to bury the child themselves and mark the grave.

As time allowed, they had gone to the nearest town to a stone mason and had the head-stone made. They returned, reliving the sorrow of those days gone by, and fixed the head-stone on the site of the grave. As I passed by, there it stood a silent witness to love, courage and endurance. I prayed that their act of going back would help to heal their broken hearts. The headstone marks an untold story of some of the wonderful people who have helped to make our country.

Jesus said in Matthew 5:4. "Blessed are those who mourn, for they shall be comforted." And another text says in 2 Corinthians 1:3-4 "The God of all comfort, who comforts us in all our tribulation."

Reflection: For the comfort that you give us in times of grief, Lord, I am truly grateful.

Life Saving Water

Re-cycled water! Because city folk now are finding they have to show some care, we hear a lot more about water shortages. When we were kids, our water was supplied by a tank which was filled with runoff water from the roof of the house when it rained. If it didn't rain before the tank was empty then we had to use bore and well water. On plenty of occasions it was what we drank, washed in and we thought it was great.

The following does not need to be practiced much, if at all, today.

When I was with a cattle mustering team in the Gulf, we were camped by a big water-hole. Cattle used it – the horses rolled in it and saddle cloths were washed in it. First thing in the morning, we went with two four-gallon kerosene tins made into buckets and filled them while the water was settled. We then took them back to camp to be boiled, one for cooking and one for drinking, which was made into black tea in order to make it look better.

Another practice which was important to know when getting a drink from a water course used by cattle was to brush the surface first, wait for the red worms to come up, for that is the way they get into the host animal's stomach. We really don't need red worms, you then wait for the worms to go back down and you are able to get your water.

While up North, a mate with more experience than me showed me how to get water out of a Tea Tree because someone had perished a few months earlier through lack of knowledge. Selecting a Tea Tree with a bump on the trunk, he cut into the knob and out came about a pannikin or mug of water. It did taste very different, but it was water, which could mean the difference between life and death.

Jesus, in a personal interview pointed out the value of water for body and soul. John 4:6-26.

Reflection: Thank you Lord that you have provided good things for us that sustain us.

Equality

During the harvest season, we had to wait in line with truck-loads of wheat at terminals, and we would swap experiences with the other truck drivers. One of the drivers had a broad scar from his hip to his knee. I said, "What on earth happened to you to have such a scar?" "Oh, I am partly German," he said, "I was smashed up during the war and taken prisoner. The doctors wanted to see if they could put a femur bone in me. There was a dying German soldier, so they took his bone out and transferred it to me and I am alive to tell the tale."

I wondered if this fellow was making up the story (fancy me being a doubter). I have since had the opportunity to ask a specialist in these matters. "Could a man recover from this operation since it was before antibiotics were available and the skills of these modern days?" He assured me that those and other such operations did happen during the war. There was, however, a high mortality rate, yet numbers of these sorts operations were successful. Most ordinary people would accept that all people are special, we need each other and ideally, we should all have an equal opportunity in life.

In Acts 17:24 ...."God that made the world and all things therein, seeing that He is Lord of heaven and earth, dwelleth not in temples made with hands; neither is worshipped with men's hands, as though He needed anything, seeing He giveth to all life, and breath, and all things; and hath made of one blood all nations of men for to dwell on all the face of the earth"

Reflection: Thank you, Lord, for being bigger than anything man can make.

Taught by Experience

There was a time when I didn't practise what I had been taught for my safety, so that I would get the best result by acknowledging a God made principle.

This I learnt when riding young horses. I was on a horse which had only been broken in to saddle for two weeks. We were following a quiet mob of cattle. The horse was relaxed and walking well. I had let the reins loose and I thought "I wonder what she'd do if I grabbed her behind the saddle?" I broke rule one by leaving the reins loose and then rule two by doing just what I had been thinking. Without warning, I grabbed her backbone behind the saddle. She only bucked once and I left her like a cork out of a bottle. I then experienced the principle of gravity 'that what goes up must come down'. Thereafter I obeyed the rules to avoid the consequences of stopping suddenly on the ground.

Jesus was asked what the greatest commandment or principle was to live by and He answered, "Thou shalt love the Lord thy God with all thy heart, and with all thy soul, and with all thy mind. This is the first and great commandment. And the second is like unto it, Thou, shalt love thy neighbour as thyself". Matthew 22:37-39.

If this was practised, what a different world it would be.

Reflection: Thank you Lord for the law of nature that applies consistently to all. Help us to follow your greatest commandment to love you and each other and to make the world a better place.

Bogged

After the war, I was fortunate enough to get employment with a 'forward thinking' station owner. He had just acquired two crawler tractors, which were small in comparison to today's machines. These were to be used for scrub pulling. This was a new approach to clearing country.

We had tried this approach at North Star in North West New South Wales and were then moving the machinery over the border to another station on the Moonie River, where working conditions were good, with a large mobile trailer with two bedrooms, kitchen and food supplied. This was new to me.

Moving the tractors there on poorly made roads of graded dirt at best, was slow going. After passing through Goondiwindi, the road became a track only. A storm had passed through and the mud brought us to a standstill. We spent the night in the vehicles, which were a table top truck with the smallest tractor on it. The bigger tractor was on a single axle semi-trailer, which was the biggest vehicle available in those days.

We had supplies to supplement the camp store which was some tin food, tea and a billy, no tin opener and no mugs. We had been drinking from the water bags. So, we opened the tins with a butcher's knife, ate the contents, washed the tins, and used them for mugs. The tins were so hot the tea had to be nearly cold before we could drink it.

Now fed, we slept as well as we could. By about 10 o'clock the next morning, we tried to move on. The semi-trailer jack-knifed, and the table top would not steer, it was still too wet. We towed the table top by chain from the back of the semi which kept it straight and the table top followed the semi for the miles until we reached the Moonie Highway, which in those days was not surfaced. Once there it was a trouble-free run to our destination.

Now with good roads, big vehicles that have comforts, such distances are covered in a few hours. Yet when it comes to the journey of life and the life hereafter, many fail to understand that Jesus Christ said, "I am the Way, the Truth, and the Life:" John 14:6.

Reflection: Thank you, Lord, for loving us enough to show us the way to go and the truth in our lives as well as the way to have eternal life.

Pulling Scrub

We pulled our trucks onto a 25,000-acre Station on which was a caretaker's home and outer buildings with a few grass flats close to the water course. All it carried was a few hundred growing steers.

The station was bought for a low price because it produced so little and was once covered with prickly pear. The Cactoblastis grubs had destroyed the pear. Now on the sandy ridges were Wilga trees and runty gum trees. The good country was covered with Brigalow scrub and a few big Belah trees. Only men with foresight, big hearts and deep pockets would dream of making it a productive property.

So, with small bulldozers which had no cabins, just a protective roof, we pushed our way out into this vast acreage of logs and scrub, and started this clearing adventure. Later, they developed bigger, better, and more comfortable machinery. In our day, it was slow, hard, and long hours of work, which made a very small impression on such a huge project.

I do not remember seeing any native life except a few along the water course. It had been a wet year, so mosquitoes, like I'd never seen, rose in clouds like black smoke whenever a bush was bumped. We wore boiler overalls, but the mosquitoes bit us through the material. When they were wiped off a fresh lot would settle where their mates had been. We discovered that mosquitoes could gorge themselves in one minute. I realized why we were provided with a good gauzed caravan for sleeping and eating.

I left that employment a few months later to study Theology. Life took on a very different aspect. My fellow students found it hard to understand my 'non city' approach, hence they nick-named me "Mulga".

Years later I understood that the property we had started to improve had become wonderfully productive. The Bible says in Proverbs

29:18, "Where there is no vision the people perish". My boss's vision certainly saved that property from dereliction.

Reflection: Lord, sometimes you give us great visions but I thank you that you often ask us to walk by faith not by sight.

Fire

Bags of wheat were stacked in the paddock ready to be loaded on to the trucks and headers were still busy bringing in the rest of the crop. Nearby a good crop of linseed waited for the headers to come and put its precious seed into bags, for it was from this crop the oil would be extracted. All workers put in long hours at harvest time, while casual employees were put on and their experience was often lacking.

One newcomer was asked to boil the billy for smoko and in his ignorance, instead of lighting the fire in a cleared area, he lit it close to the stubble where the tucker box had been left. The fire was soon into the wheat and then into the linseed crop with its seeds full of oil which sent the fire flashing over hundreds of acres in minutes and then into the scrub. Machines were moved to safety fast and neighbours stopped their harvesting, coming from miles around and spent the rest of the day and night trying to contain the fire. I don't remember what happened to the casual employee.

This was an occasion which showed how a little fire can become the cause of great damage as the wheat stack burned for days and was a complete loss.

In the Bible, the book of James 3:6 warns that the tongue, like a fire, can cause so much evil. But he also says in Verse 17 that Wisdom from above is first pure, peaceable, and gentle.

I have made lots of mistakes with my tongue, but now, with God's help, I endeavour to use this powerful member of the body for good.

Reflection: Thank you Father, that you can send your spirit to those who ask, to make us burn with a passion that can only come from you.

God Giveth.

In the 1940's when our family was farming, the tractors were powered by what was called power kerosene. It was quite an art to start them. First, all the kerosene had to be drained out of the carburettor and petrol turned on from a small tank. With a crank handle, the engine was turned over by hand until it started. When the engine heated up, you turned the power kerosene over from the big tank, not forgetting to turn off the small petrol tank.

You could then work for the day, as long as you kept the engine hot. If you stopped, say for lunch, the starting process had to be completed all over again. During the war, when petrol was rationed and hard to get, the motors were often left running even while the kerosene tank was being filled.

One farmer was doing just that with a four-gallon drum, when it overflowed on to the hot engine and exploded, burning him extensively. His brother was riding away on his horse after having delivered him a message. He had a compelling urge to go back to his brother.

He arrived just as the explosion occurred. The only way he could extinguish the flames on his brother was to roll him in the soft ploughed soil. Then he urgently needed to get him to hospital, which was a much slower trip in those days. When he was finally admitted to hospital, he was delirious with the pain. For weeks he hung between life and death. The family was able to secure the services of a trained nurse to care for him continually. His Christian friends believe that because of their prayers they had seen God intervene and his life was restored when it looked impossible. It was obvious that he would never be able to do the physical work of farming again.

Now he was faced with the decision, "To what could he apply himself?" He took on a small agency and auctioneering business which became very progressive and opened up other business opportunities with many employees and sub-contractors, as well as becoming a local Councillor.

Out of tragedy and injury grew something special. The Hymn writer puts it this way;
When we have exhausted our store of endurance,
when our strength has failed ere the day is half-done,
When we reach the end of our hoarded resources
our Father's full giving is only begun.

His love has no limits, His grace has no measure,
His power no boundary known unto men;
For out of His infinite riches in Jesus
He giveth, and giveth, and giveth again."

Reflection: Oh, how wonderful it is that your resources are infinite, Lord.

[1] He Giveth More Grace by Annie Johnson Flint verses 2 & 4

Making Hay

When horses were being put aside and tractors and machines were taking over, there was much converting of horse drawn machinery to tractors. Instead of many chains and bars, there was just one hitch. This happened on our farm. Our first tractor had steel wheels and large studs to stop it slipping. The engine was started by a crank handle, which required some skill and muscle to get it working. There was no self-starter or light. When we needed to work during the night, a lighted kerosene lantern was hung on the front of the tractor. A full moon was certainly a big help. Hay cutting was done at our place by a contractor who still had horses, a reaper and binder.

It mowed the wheat or oats, took it up on a moving six-foot sheet of canvas to the inner workings of the binder. It then tied the wheat into bundles, called sheaves, and flicked them out on to the ground. We then had to go around, putting them into stooks of ten or more sheaves, heads facing up, the knot being placed on the inside, so the rain would not stay in the indent that the knot had left. These were left to dry out, or until a haystack builder came. In our time, a good stack builder was rare and we had to get one from sixty-five kilometres away. We converted a horse wagon to be pulled by a tractor to pick up the stooks to go to the haystack. There was a tractor driver, a man on the wagon stacking the sheaves (one year, the man's name was Darcy, a real old timer and great fun to work with), and a man on the ground to throw up the sheaves using a long handled pitch fork. The stooks were often left in the paddock for weeks, thus there were field mice in the sheaves and occasionally a snake. Up went a snake in a sheaf to Darcy. We called in alarm, "There's a snake gone up, Darcy!" He looked over the top of the load some ten feet up and said, with a smile, "Don't worry, I'll clean his ear with the pitch fork!"

We took the load to the hay stack. The haystack builder finished the stacks in a way which made them water proof and would last until they were ready to be cut into chaff. We warned the builder about the snake, but we do not know what became of it as it was not seen again. These old ways and skill of storing hay have been superseded by baling machines, but the commitment to do work efficiently is what makes for happy and fulfilling personalities.

Philippians 4:13, says "I can do all things through Christ who strengthens me."

Reflection: Thank you Father for giving us the strength to do all that is required of us by you.

Bulls

Bulls were always an important part of farm life, before artificial insemination, which now provides access to the best available bulls. I was told, "Never trust a bull, because you can never be sure when they might charge." We experienced the tragedy of my sister's son, who was a first-class shearer, rough rider, and cattle transport driver, being killed by a bull while he was loading cattle in a stock yard. Because he was so well known and respected, the Town Hall was used for the funeral and an estimated 3,000 people attended.

During the early war years, one of Dad's friends had a Land Army girl helping with the dairy work. When she went to bring the cows in for the afternoon milking, the bull charged her. Fortunately, she was able to roll under the fence and escape badly shaken and bruised.

The owner called Dad for help, stating that they would kill the bull that night. Having trouble getting him into the yard, he used a pitch fork to drive him in and declared, "He's in the yard now". The war was on, so there was no rifle available to shoot him and I decline to tell of the method used. However, the next week, he was boiled down for pig feed.

Having been warned in my youth to never trust a bull and never to be careless when working with them, I should have behaved differently. It was a bull which caused me to experience real fear. We'd had this bull since he was twelve months old and always kept him in a separate bull yard. We fed him every day, cows were put in with him for service and he'd never showed any signs of a bad temper. I was working in his yard and took my concentration off him. I never saw him coming until he knocked me to the ground and was coming back the second time with head down (he was dehorned) ready to push and trample me into the ground. He was so close that I poked my fingers into his eyes and screamed with fear.

I didn't realize that I had such a shrill voice, but it brought our workman nearby to help.

Because of that fearful experience, I have remembered that advice to never let down your guard while working with a bull.

Jesus warned that there would be times when, to be a believer of Christ could cost us our lives, creating fear, He said to His followers, "Be not afraid of them that kill the body .... For are not five sparrows sold for two copper coins and not one of them is forgotten before God. But the very hairs of your head are numbered – do not fear therefore, you are of more value than many sparrows." Luke 12:4-7, New King James Version.

Reflection: For the protection of our spiritual and physical bodies, oh God, we thank you.

In a Bar

As a Salvation Army Officer, I often visited local establishments in uniform. On one occasion I met a prominent citizen, a First World War Veteran, whom I knew from meeting on public occasions. At weekends he had his drinks. One Saturday I walked into the bar that he frequented. He deliberately came over to me, put his arm around my shoulder and said, 'You're a lovely old bastard. Oops! I should not talk to a 'Man of the Cloth' that way." Then he added, "In Australia that's a term of endearment." What prompted that I do not know – obviously he approved of what I stood for.

Like this visit and many others, I got to see that issues with alcohol are not the domain of just one group of people. It can affect anyone. In Ephesians 5:18 the Bible tells us "and be not drunk with wine wherein is excess; but be filled with the spirit."

The spirit that the Bible verse is referring to is God's Spirit. To be filled with His Spirit we need to first come to Jesus and ask Him into our lives. We can do this because He came to earth, died on the cross, rose again, and returned to Heaven.

Proverbs 18:24 says, "A man that hath friends must show himself friendly: and there is a friend that sticketh closer than a brother." Jesus is that friend who wants to be your brother.

Reflection: I am eternally grateful, Lord, that you love all of mankind, no matter where they live or how they live.

Caring

One minister who taught me a lot about caring for people was a man who achieved much but never gave the impression of being in a hurry. When we knew him, he had a congregation of about five hundred families and cared for another little congregation of about twenty families in a village about sixty kilometres away. He believed the Bible was true and the instruction book for a happy, creative, and fulfilling life and spoke it forcefully. There were those who didn't agree with him, yet he really cared for people when things in their lives were hard.

In the little village a tragedy struck. A young couple's marriage broke up. The man felt he had lost all that he had lived for and committed suicide. That can happen when one feels there is no one to love and no one cares. At any bereavement one feels inadequate to really enter into their sorrow and loss but tries to share as much as possible. The mother of the deceased was devastated as only mothers can be. When the minister heard, he drove the sixty kilometres to share with the mother. Whatever he said or did, it started her healing process, long and slow as it was. Years after, a friend cautiously asked, "What did our minister say to you?" Her reply was "Nothing that I can remember, but he came, held my hand and cried with me." No doubt he prayed and did other Christian things, yet it is not what is said that people remember, but how you make them feel.

In the Bible we read about when Jesus went to two sisters who were bereaved. He entered into their grief. In the Gospel of John 11:35 it says "Jesus wept." They knew He understood.

Reflection: I thank you, Lord Jesus, for the knowledge that, because you walked through our world, you understand how we feel.

What a Friend

Some years ago, I had to travel quite a long distance to conduct a funeral service at a crematorium. I arrived early and there were few vehicles about. As I needed time to ready myself for the service, I drove to the end of the parking lot and sat quietly to relax. I viewed the trimmed shrubs and manicured lawns with marble plates marking where families had paid a tribute to loved ones. It was a credit to those responsible.

A car pulled in nearby, and out stepped a well-kept man who purposely walked to one of the marble plates and knelt in front of it. I felt I was viewing something very personal. I dare not get out or open my car door, lest I disturb this special occasion. Was it sorrow, love expressed, loneliness, a lost wife, child, or mother? After ten minutes or so he rose, head bent, returned to his car, and was gone.

Yet it is, forever etched on my memory. How I wanted to tell him what Joseph Scriven had written:

What a Friend we have in Jesus,
All our sins and griefs to bear!
What a privilege to carry
Everything to God in prayer!
O what peace we often forfeit,
O what needless pain we bear,
All because we do not carry
Everything to God in prayer!

Reflection: Thank you, Lord, for being the friend that we can come to at any time of the day or night, and you will be there for us.

Discipline

I am a great believer in the wonderful capacity of our young people to achieve great things both mentally and physically.

However, one of my concerns is that before experience has taught them the essentials of participating in the work force, some of them don't receive the balanced information needed to have a fulfilling life and thus improve our great country.

We were travelling interstate a few years ago and spent a few days with friends. They were giving hospitality to a young man in his late teens, who had a fine physique and appeared quite intelligent. He questioned us about the early days of country life. When I mentioned that, at times, we bathed once or twice a week in order to conserve water, he was horrified, and said, "I must shower every day, that is hygiene!"

But about his ambitions for life, he could give no goals he had in mind, and had not had any jobs of any duration. He had no discipline of mind or body when it came to work. His hygiene was disciplined, yet his unbalanced way of life made for a boy who was unsettled in himself and a worry to those who cared about him.

I now understand that there must be some work to receive benefits. I also believe that such young people are in the minority. We all could learn from Herman Cain's philosophy –
"Every job is a good job, that's where you start" – and

> Life is just a minute, only 60 seconds in it,
> Forced upon you, couldn't refuse it,
> Didn't seek it, didn't choose it
> But it's up to you to use it.
> You must suffer if you lose it,
> Give an account if you abuse it.
> Just a tiny little minute,

But eternity is in it.

We also need to learn the Bible truth, "The sleep of a labouring man is sweet, whether he eat little or much." Ecclesiastes 5:12.

Reflection: I praise you that we are able to experience the benefits of working regardless of whether we get paid or not.

Found Out and Seeing Clearly

Ministers are trained in Biblical Studies, public speaking, and a number of other aspects of public relations. Nothing, however, can take the place of the experience of meeting people in the place of their real need.

I knew of an inexperienced young Minister in an inner Sydney suburb when that part of the city was rather run down. Doing visitation, he came to one lady who offered him a cup of tea, which he accepted.

When the tea was put down, he saw that the cup was dirty, and the tea did not look the best. When the lady left the room, he decided to throw the contents out a nearby window. The window was closed – the glass being much cleaner than the cup. He had to confess and clean up the mess, the result of him jumping to the wrong conclusions.

One saying we sometimes use in our home is, "The only exercise some people get is jumping to conclusions." We should not do this when we meet people as we cannot clean up the damage done to others as easily as that mess made by the cup of tea was. We need to remember the Bible says in 1 Samuel 16:7 b "The Lord does not see as man sees; for man looks on the outward appearance, but the Lord looks at the heart." Experience can teach you what can't be learnt from books.

The Bible says in Numbers 32:23 ...... "Be sure your sins (or misdeeds) will find you out".

Reflection: I thank you that your lessons in life come in many forms.

Three Blind Mice (or Dead Mice)

I do not always feel proud of some of my actions or of some of my colleagues. Some things bring shame on Christianity while others are just unkind pranks.

One Minister went to visit an old lady who had a piano which had not been played for many years. The lady asked if he could play the piano. He was a gifted musician, so said he would try. He ran his fingers along the keys, noticing that something was not right. He lifted the top lid and found an old rat's nest, which he removed to the lady's surprise. It then played a little better. His sense of humour came to the fore and he played very slowly, "Three blind mice, see how they run." He assumed there was very little knowledge of Church Hymns when the lady, with clasped hands and a heavenly gaze, said, "Oh Rev. aren't the old hymns lovely."

Isn't it wonderful that God doesn't jump to conclusions and look on outward appearances, but knows what we really are?

The Bible says in 1 Samuel 16:7 "....The Lord does not see as man sees; for man looks at the outward appearance, but the Lord looks at the heart."

Reflection: I thank you Lord for knowing me so completely inside and out.

Outback Chaplaincy

Being married in the 1950's, we set off to our first Church as a newly married couple. We travelled by car to Mt Isa, I say by car, as there were places where there were no roads. We did it in three days, putting a hole in the petrol tank, changing one wheel and a few stops when the heat had caused the petrol to evaporate. This meant that the electric pump stopped. We do not remember meeting any other vehicles on the way, yet it was quite a good trip. The isolation was intense, we had no communication.

As we viewed Mt Isa from a distance we stopped and prayed for wisdom and guidance. We had no idea how much this would be needed. Our district that we were responsible for went west to Camooweal, south to Kynuna, east to Richmond, north to Normanton and back to the Northern Territory border.

Today the roads are good, and communications are amazing to us 'oldies'. But with all the modern advances today, I believe people feel more alone and forgotten than ever. This was a problem that John Flynn recognised and there are many people who still work today to help these people to feel connected. We may not know their names but we can still pray and ask God to give them strength and energy to carry out His work.

Deuteronomy 16:17 says, "Every man shall give as he is able, according to the blessing of the Lord your God which He has given you."

Reflection: Lord, so many of your people look to you for strength, courage, and power to spread your gospel, I thank you that you are faithfully helping those you have called.

Meeting People

Over fifty years ago, mining towns such as Mt Isa, were places where the wages were large and the bonuses were extra. Many wonderful people lived there and others came to town because they believed that more money and bonuses would solve their problems.

They forgot that they brought their characters and personalities with them, which meant that more money certainly did not mean improved morals. Wealth did not give wisdom and the imagination only limits the 'goings on'.

Our home was partitioned rooms on the back of a white-ant eaten timber church, cement floor, no lining or ceiling, outback washhouse and further out the pan toilet. Air flowed through all the gaps which were part of the building structure bringing with it plenty of dust to stick to the perspiration. Roads in town were dusty tracks with very little bitumen. However, we were better off than many others.

My young wife was so gracious. At the start she put out some of our wedding gifts but realized they would soon be ruined by those conditions, so packed them away again for those years. It felt a lot like we were camping, not setting up a new home. We had to learn what Theological Seminary didn't teach us and that is that you had to concentrate on the needs of the people, and they were many, not on our own comfort. We were experiencing that, in the spiritual service of the people, we often have to go without, just as athletes need to do to achieve the goals they set.

Paul wrote in 1 Corinthians 9:25 – "Every athlete in training submits to strict discipline, in order to be crowned with a wreath that will not last; but we do it for one that will last forever."

Reflection: I thank you that, no matter what we have to do without here on earth, Lord, you will faithfully give us so much more, full measure, pressed down, and running over.

Peace

In Luke 2:14, the angels sang "Glory to God in the highest, and on earth peace, good will toward men."

Peace was often shattered in isolated mining towns in the 1950's because of overcrowded accommodation. Costs were high. Single galvanized car garages to live in would cost twenty-five Pounds ($50) per week. Six beds under a high house would be sold singularly for the night's sleep. Any shelter was worth money. There was no Government shelter for those put out of accommodation.

On one weekend, three different women came for shelter. We have forgotten the details of two of them, but the third was a mother who had piggy-backed her small child for about a mile in the dark. Both were emotionally upset. So, we needed to provide some shelter and security for them, hope but hardly peace.

Jesus said in John 14:27, "Peace I leave with you, My peace I give to you; not as the world gives do I give to you. Let not your heart be troubled, neither let it be afraid."

The world struggles to give peace by making rules, laws, and shelters which is commendable, yet it is the inner peace of the spirit, emotions, and soul which Jesus gives and which the entire world's assets, credits and accolades cannot give. Jesus' peace brings the real spirit of Christmas. May your Christmas have all the joys you strive for, but do not forget to add Jesus' Peace.

Reflection: Oh Lord, I am so grateful for the peace that you give us in the midst of the world's troubles.

Mozzies come to Church

Red dust was a part of living in Mt Isa, as were the whirly-gigs that could lift any loose articles high into the air! If your residence was in their pathway, what a mess was left for you to sweep up.

Atomiser Fly Sprayer - Photo courtesy of Kilkivan Museum Queensland

In those days, mining left stagnant water pools so, added to the dust, mosquitoes thrived in plague proportions. Buildings open for air flow gave free access to insects. The best way to sleep was under a mosquito net. This was a very large piece of netting which was hung from a pole above the bed and it was big enough to be tucked in like your sheets to create a small tent like arrangement. You got in and then sprayed the mosquitoes which got in with you with the old atomizer spray pump – then put the pump out trying not to let any more of the suckers in. There were no Pressure Packs in those days.

People now want all sorts of convenience in churches. How I respect the worshippers of those days. You would spray around the congregation at the commencement of the service, killing Mosquito wave number 1. Then half way through there would be a pause as wave number 2 attacked, so spray again, and then on to the latter half of the service. That meant no long sermons. Another way of escaping these attacks was for the ladies to sit Buddha style covering their legs with their skirts. They didn't wear slacks in those days and men gladly wore long trousers. Worship over, we swept up the mosquitoes in dust pans full, then pushed the pews back to make room for mattresses for people to sleep on when they could not find lodging for the night. When people come to worship under such conditions it was important that they received spiritual strength to cope with daily life.

The Bible says, in Philippians 4:6-7 "Be anxious for nothing, but in everything, by prayer and supplication, with thanksgiving, let your requests be made known to God; and the peace of God, which surpasses all understanding, will guard your hearts and minds through Christ Jesus".

Reflection: Lord we thank you for all your creatures even if you are the only one that knows their purpose in our world.

Is this Texas

Housing shortages in boom towns! This is not a new problem.

A tradesman from a quiet coastal village came to the mining town of Mt Isa while we were living there. He was having trouble getting suitable accommodation. He came to us to see if it was possible to have a mattress on the church floor at night.

The following is part of his experience: He had a job, great pay and had slept for a fortnight at the Railway Station. Then a room became available at the local hotel. He thought that would be good! On his first night there, the Police had been given a 'tip off' about a group who were planning to 'knock off' the hotel's safe containing the 'takings'.

The law enforcement powers arranged for the owner to fill the safe with pennies, giving the impression of a big haul. Late at night the thieves struck. They were on their way to the 'get away' vehicle with their weighty haul when the Police called on them to stop. 'No way!' they were not letting go of this great find. The Police had no option but to use their firearms a number of times. Our tradesman said, "I thought I was in Texas!" so he moved out. He said that our primitive sleeping arrangements would be fine. He was lonely away from his wife and family, so we shared supper with him.

We remember that the Bible says in Hebrews 13:2, "Be not forgetful to entertain strangers: for thereby some have entertained angels unawares."

Reflection: Oh Lord, please help us to remember to look for your wonders in the tough situations of life.

Sleeping Rough

At Mt Isa we had a lot of men using the Church for temporary sleeping shelter while they were looking for alternative accommodation. One tradesman was told by a workmate that he would be welcome to a bed at his place. He decided to accept the offer. We thought this would be an improvement to sleeping on the Church floor, but he was back the following night.

This is what happened: His mate's buildings were temporary and the accommodation was rough although the bed was OK. The water came from a make-shift town supply piped first to one residence in the area. They filled their forty-four-gallon drum, turned off the tap which allowed the water to go on to the next neighbour, who would do the same, and so on down the line. This was the only drinking and washing water available.

As night approached, the owners and neighbours gathered to slake their thirst with all their beer before bed, as there was no refrigeration. Our tradesman thought this was all a bit rough, with some of the guests being of doubtful character. To protect his money, he put it into a sock and tied it to his pyjama cord. This kept it safe from wrong hands.

Next morning the husband had to go to work. He got up, asked his wife to get breakfast, went to the forty-four and filled his dish for his morning ablutions. By now the wife, still sluggish from the previous night's party, had not moved. So 'Hubby' threw the dish full of used soapy water over 'Wifey' while she was still in bed to get her moving, which she did with a very colourful description of her man's character. The tradesman realized this arrangement was unsatisfactory, but appreciated their kindness and thanked them.

The Bible says in Proverbs 22:3, "Sensible people will see trouble coming and avoid it." So, he was back the next day to use the Church to sleep in until something better came along.

Reflection: Please give us eyes to see danger before we fall, oh Lord.

Getting on the Sauce

When men rushed to mining towns, finding accommodation was difficult. One man found he could get a bed under a house with the five other men who were already there. However, they had to find tucker somewhere else. There was a provider of meals and packed lunches in town, which is where these men went. The food was basic but plentiful. The meat was steak cooked on top of a large shearer's oven much like our modern barbeques, served with mashed potatoes and other veggies when available.

The Proprietor was the cook. He was an amply built man wearing a wrap-around calico apron showing the marks of wear over his front. A couple of ladies worked as waitresses and packed the lunches. The ten tables, each seating four people, were bare except for the adornment of salt and pepper and a bottle of Worcestershire Sauce. There was no gravy served so the sauce was their only option. As there was no alternative place for breakfast, business was usually very good.

Things went well except when Cliff, a heavy alcoholic drinker, recovering from a night's 'bender' would quietly come, whip off some sauce bottles and drink the contents to help his craving. It was expected that any customer, seeing Cliff coming, was to call out to the waitresses, "Here comes Cliff". There was then a hurried removal of all sauce bottles from the tables. These were returned to the tables only with the individual meals. The men were thus fed for the day's work. Such basic food providers have now disappeared.

The Prophets of the Bible understood Cliff's problem and wrote in Isaiah 5:11, "Woe unto them that rise up early in the morning, that they may follow strong drink; that continue until night, till wine inflame them."

Reflection: Lord, I am so grateful that when you hear our pleas for healing, you heal completely.

A Drunk Preacher

Alcohol is a drink which is used by people who have different needs and for lots of different reasons. It is used at weddings, at a birth to celebrate the new life, at death to get people through sorrow, when they feel alone, when in a crowd, or when they need courage. It makes some people sing but it makes some angry. I was taught, "A drunken man speaks a sober man's mind."

With all the different actions and reactions, it causes, only once did I know it to make a man preach. Cliff, from the previous story, preached when he became intoxicated. Because of this I was somehow identified with him. The boys at the pub would shout him drinks, put him up on the bar and he would preach. He would be theologically sound. He called for repentance using verses like Acts 3:19 "Repent therefore and be converted, that your sins may be blotted out." And for Salvation he quoted John 3:16, "For God so loved the world that He gave His only begotten Son, that whoever believes in Him should not perish but have everlasting life."

The boys would give him more drink and he would continue to preach with increased vigour. I wondered what the reason was behind Cliff's behaviour. I'll tell how we found out some of his story on the next page. Only God knows what his preaching did for others who heard God's truth.

Reflection: Oh Lord, how we thank you that we do not get to know all that you manage to do through our good deeds or even our mistakes.

A Drunken Preacher Sober

Because Cliff preached when he was drunk, many thought I should know of his whereabouts. This was unknown to me, yet I was desirous of helping him whenever possible. Someone came one day and told us that Cliff was really in a bad way and had crawled under the railway goods shed. A mate and I took the ute and went to investigate. There he was. We pulled him out, put him in the back of the ute and took him home to our place.

Care facilities for such cases were poor. I had no 'hands on' experience with men in this condition. However, I remembered my father telling me some of his experience. He had worked for a wonderful tradesman who would often go on an alcohol bender, and when he was recovering his wife gave him soup. So, my good wife fed Cliff soup. We also tried to encourage him to get God's help to overcome the drink demon. It took some time for him to get his strength back. We gave him odd jobs to do around the Church; he left the drink alone and became reliable.

This was his story: He came from New Zealand where he had a responsible job. A bad motor bike accident had left him with severe head injuries. He had a plate inserted during the operation as part of his recovery. This explained his sometimes-unusual behaviour and alcohol addiction. When we take the trouble to know what people have gone through, we are able to show so much more understanding.

Cliff did well, getting a job and accommodation at the mines, which had never happened before, he now had money and was planning to go home to New Zealand for Christmas. Unfortunately, there are always bad men as well as good. Some of the crooks realized Cliff had money. They forced drink into him and he was off again into his unreal world. They took his money so he never went to New Zealand. He lost his job and his quality of life.

This is one of the disappointments of dealing with people. When needing encouragement, the Bible says in Philippians 4:6 "Be anxious for nothing, but in everything by prayer and supplication, with thanksgiving, let your requests be made known to God."

Reflection: We thank you, Lord, for your love of all mankind.

A Wise Woman

A mining town is usually known as a 'man's domain', yet there have been some very remarkable women who have made significant contributions to such areas. One such woman, with two fine boys almost in their teens, came to our Worship Services. Her story was one of courage.

She had come from Canada, following a family tragedy, hoping that a tour of this great country of Australia would prove to be a therapy for herself and her boys. They had visited many places before arriving in our mining town, only to experience a severe housing shortage. She decided to build her own home. After going through the proper channels, she built a cement brick house, doing most of the work herself while the boys were at school. Her plan was to eventually sell for a profit and in the meantime have somewhere to live while in Australia.

When the time came to return to Canada, the healing of the boys' trauma had been accomplished and the house building helped to defray the cost of their Australian adventure.

The Bible speaks of such a mother in Proverbs 31:26-28.
"She opens her mouth with wisdom, and on her tongue is the law of kindness. She watches over the ways of her household, and does not eat the bread of idleness. Her children rise up and call her blessed...."

Reflection: We thank you that you give wisdom to both men and women.

Texas

In remote parts of Australia, you find men living who have come from different backgrounds and with a variety of experiences. You only listen to the stories that are volunteered, for they want to live as people without a past. In northwest Queensland, a man known as 'Texas' would periodically come to Mt Isa from the Northern Territory to drink his accumulated wages.

He must have been accustomed to hard physical work, because he was a wonderful specimen of a man, tall, muscles rippled on every limb and his ribs were like rafters. He tied his shirt in a knot over his navel so you saw his massive chest. He had a 'stand out' personality to match his physique.

He was the only man I have met who could drink his beer by throwing his head back and pouring the liquid down his throat. It just went straight down without his Adams Apple appearing to even move. He would stay in town while his wages lasted, then come down to us for money for a meal. Of course, money for a meal was not his real need and we would have happily have provided a meal. With no money forthcoming, he would go off, mostly returning in a few days with another story, because he had run out of financial helpers elsewhere. I then suggested that he hand himself over to the police, who would put him in on vagrancy till he dried out, then he could take the mail truck back to his job. When his wages had accumulated again, we'd see him back in town again.

Proverbs 20:29 says, "The glory of young men is their strength" and Isaiah 40:31 says, "But they that wait upon the Lord shall renew their strength."

Reflection: For the strength you give us when we are weak, we thank you, Lord.

The Mysteries of God's Working

I had known this young couple back in the 1960's and christened their children, but could not have foreseen the international activities in which they would participate. Colin and Aileen Cavanagh were the special guests of the Union Church one weekend in March. When Aileen was 37 years old, a heart disease caused a heart attack. Tests showed a progressive, deteriorating condition. At this early age, the emotions of fear and the discouragement over of not completing a fulfilling life flooded in. To those who do not know God, it is a dark and devastating experience. Yet for Colin and Aileen, they were to start an unexpected life change.

Aileen woke one night with the urge to read Isaiah 45:3, "I will give you the treasures of darkness and hidden riches of secret places that you may know that I, the Lord, Who call you by your name, am the God of Israel." Really feeling that God had touched her life, she felt improvement and requested further testing. The Doctors could not explain the improvement. With medication, no more running and using lifts instead of stairs, life was progressively improving.

They moved to Queensland, into the hospitality industry. Aileen worked with the Christian Organization 'Aglow Australia', attending seven of their International Conferences in the U.S.A. Up to 11,000 women gathered from 160 countries around the world where they were able to encourage each other in their spiritual lives. At one conference, she was privileged to be the Australian Standard Bearer in the 150-flag parade. Travels have taken her to other countries of the world and different parts of Australia. She has also made time to complete a diploma in Counselling.

Within a few months of retiring, they became restless. Over twelve months ago another business opportunity was offered to them and they now have a staff of thirteen and life is full on again. When we realize that God knows our names and has a special care for us, life is great.

Reflection: Oh Lord, I am so grateful that you know my name and have a great plan for me.

The Silent Passenger

Mary Kathleen Uranium Mine has been worked out and the town dismantled. However, when I had driven into it from Cloncurry in my ministry early days, the contractors were just starting work on the village. There were offices for the manager and planners, plus one tent used by the machinery operator and his family. This was well set up with timber floor and separate sleeping area. The manager was happy to see me. He said "You are the first Minister we have seen." We discussed the spiritual needs they expected to transpire.

Accommodation and entertainment were in the planning stages and they were endeavouring to avoid many of the mistakes made by other early mining towns. They didn't want a shanty town growing up around the township. When their workers arrived, they wanted them to have adequate accommodation. He then said, "We had a man hike in this morning and we don't want him staying. Could you take him back to Mt. Isa?"

The drive was about sixty kilometres and took two hours because of the rough patches and bull dust. It was quite a slow exercise, but being late getting away we needed to hurry with extreme care. When the passenger arrived, he was pleasant enough but obviously a city man, no swag but a large port which he put in the back of the truck and climbed in with me. Off we went, and from the turnoff the track was rough, up steep grades which dropped away without a clear view of what was ahead and plenty of sharp bends. The wipers had to be frequently used to clear the bull dust from the windshield.

Whether it was this new terrain or my bad driving, I'm not sure, but I don't remember him speaking a word from the turnoff until we pulled up in the Isa in one and a half hours. He jumped out, hauled his port from the back of the truck, hurried across the road, and half way to the hotel stopped, turned, waved and shouted, "Thank you! Thank you!" That was the last I saw of him.

If he was a praying man, he could have been using the verses of Psalm 121:7-8. "The Lord shall preserve you from all evil; He shall preserve your soul. The Lord shall preserve your going out and your coming in from this time forth, and even for evermore."

Reflection: I thank you, Lord, that you do preserve us no matter where we are in this world.

Prisoner

Transport and communication! How it has changed our way of living. Now foods come from all over the country and the world.

We are told "Fresh is best" yet in my early years, the market gardeners grew and delivered our produce, the butcher killed and brought the meat to our door, and if the milk was not delivered warm it was considered 'not fresh.' How we have changed the meaning of the word FRESH.

Church preaching opportunities have changed also. When crowds waited to go to the movies and when hotels had early closing time, the bars were full. This brought crowds of people together and the Church people would hold an open-air service with Gospel songs, stories of how God had changed lives and messages from the Bible. Favourite hymns were sung by the crowd and to help them, each verse was read out before it was sung. Many re-lived their past Church experiences as memories came back.

On one occasion, a hotel bar was full to overflowing and the old hymn "Oh for a thousand tongues to sing my great Redeemer's praise" was being sung. A small man in the bar, having had too much to drink, thought he was much bigger than he really was and was causing a lot of trouble. The police were called to take him away in handcuffs. The open-air church service had reached the last verse of that hymn which says, "He (Jesus) breaks the power of cancelled sin, **He sets the prisoner free.**" Out of the door came the tall policeman with his little man and pointing down to his prisoner's head, said in a loud voice, "Not this **prisoner!**" The service went on to tell the crowd that it's the inner man which must change by God's love before the outward results can be shown to those who know them best.

Reflection: Oh, how great you are, Lord, to be able to set us free from all those things that would make us slaves.

Sleeping in Peace

When we lived at Mt Isa, I had to be away on trips, sometimes up to ten days at a time. On these occasions I was blessed with a good and brave wife. Once she had a twelve-year-old girl staying with her for company. There was always someone needing temporary accommodation in the church or needing a meal. My wife did her best in providing for them.

One evening, the police rang to say they had a young woman on a vagrancy charge and could my wife put the lass up. She said, "Not really, there are already several men in the church and a married couple in the spare room." They said they would try elsewhere. Later they rang again to say they were unsuccessful. My wife explained the situation again. By the third time they rang, they were getting quite desperate. The cells were full of men so the young woman could not go there and all other options were 'no go'.

My wife told them to bring her down. The twelve-year-old girl had been sleeping in a camp bed in the general-purpose area, so my wife decided to move her into the double bed with herself, so the police's visitor could have the camp bed. When they arrived, the young woman, who was of ample proportions and tough looking, accepted the camp bed and settled in. She emptied her bag onto a small table and among her things was a pistol, small enough to fit into a handbag. Why hadn't the police taken possession of that was a bit of a mystery!

My wife decided to put the twelve-year-old on the farther side of the bed, so if there was any shooting she would be protected. She then put herself and the girl into God's care and had a good night's sleep. In the morning the young woman went for a wash, and my wife saw the pistol opened as a cosmetic case. She could have wasted a good night's sleep, and it shows that confidence in God does bring peace.

Psalm 4:8 says, "I will both lay me down in peace, and sleep; for Thou, Lord, only makest me dwell in safety."

Reflection: We can be so grateful, Father, that you see through everything that may not be what it seems, particularly when it comes to us human beings.

A Visitor

One of my superiors had our Church on his itinerary in connection with an investigation tour he was undertaking. He had an impressive background. He had worked in France and spoke fluent French but not the type people called "french" when swearing. He had been a Bible College Principal and was a gifted musician. He had had responsibility for a Church in a densely populated area in England with multi-story housing units. He could stand on a landing and knock on several doors at the same time. Therefore, we knew he would have trouble understanding Australian distances and culture.

We wrote him a letter giving him instructions. When he arrived in Cloncurry, he had instructions to ask directions of the town carpenter who was also the Undertaker and connected with our Church. This was because I had to travel about two hours over a very rough track from Mt Isa to meet him at Cloncurry and could well mean that I might have been delayed. However, I was there when the train arrived. He said, "Why would you ask the Station Master to direct you to the town carpenter?" He did not understand that, in outback towns, everybody knew each other.

We had an interview at the Flying Doctor Centre and with the Mine Manager, before leaving for Mt Isa. On the way we called to see a family who had started a market garden at a permanent water hole. Their housing was rough and certainly not up to the standard of his "multi-story units". We then drove through the red dust to have lunch, arranged by the ladies of the Church. Our buildings were two military huts, joined together with the Church in the front and our residence in the back, which only had cubicles and no ceiling.

We showed him the cubicle where he would be sleeping. Before he cleaned up, his eyes were framed with red dust. He said, "Poor

Norm! Living like this!" My good wife didn't even get a mention, and it was more difficult for her.

He did his part well. He was great with his music and he put a real effort into his contact with the people both young and old. It was three days before the next train left, so there was time for interviews with the local mine and civic leaders, and on the Saturday, we held an old fashioned barbeque. In those days a large fire was built in which potatoes and onions, wrapped in foil, were cooked in the ashes. Smaller fires were lit around, on which families placed a metal plate and cooked their meat.

Our visitor continued to share his music and participated in five services on Saturday and Sunday before it was time for him to go. He looked at me sternly and asked, "Did you put on all this, especially for me?" I don't think it ever dawned on him that we did this and more all the time. When there are many needs, every day brings new challenges and different activities.

Luke 9:62; "Jesus said unto him, No man, having put his hand to the plough, and looking back, is fit for the kingdom of God."

Reflection: Lord, how wonderful it is that you understand us and our needs more than any man.

A Working Holiday

In the early days, mining town workers' weekly wages were roughly $40 plus a $40 bonus a week. We were on $16 plus accommodation. Our programme covered all aspects of life, callers for help, children, youth and family activities, alcoholic meetings, and Sunday worship. We were busy.

I was late with my post graduate studies and needed to get away to catch up on my assignments. Two week's holidays were due, but with our salary, where do you go? We decided to go camping. The most available facility was the stock watering bores along the highway, which were about twenty miles apart.

We selected one bore with some shady shrubs, parked our vehicle and set up a large canvas 'lean to' for added protection. Our comforts consisted of stretchers, a table and chairs, a lantern for light, a camp fire for cooking, but there was no phone or any other form of communication, so I could concentrate on my assignments. Some friends delivered the gear in their truck, and a week later, brought fresh supplies.

Our showers were taken beside the stock water tank. We put a hose into the tank and syphoned the water out. The road was quite a distance away and as there was very little traffic, there was very little risk of anyone being able to see anything from there. However, one of us would watch while the other showered. The startled cattle didn't embarrass us.

What we had not bargained on was the interruption of some native bees. As the temperature rose, I perspired; the bees found something desirable in my moisture and came in their hundreds to drink my perspiration. With my hands occupied with writing the many pages required, my unfortunate wife spent hours during the last few days in fanning away the native bees. We knew that I had to finish the studies while we were out there, because once we were back in town, the interruptions would be continuous.

Today, education facilities and conditions are great, but I wonder about the motivation. If the motivation is there, one will achieve in spite of adverse conditions.

Paul urges us in 2 Timothy 2:15 to "Study to show thyself approved unto God, a workman that needeth not to be ashamed, rightly dividing the word of truth."

Reflection: Let our love for you be our motivation for the work that you give us to do.

A Night-time Visitor

Mt Isa Salvation Army Hall 1956

In an outback town, the temporary accommodation which we provided in our Church varied, the largest number of people staying on one night was sixteen. We stored the mattresses in a shed which had no door. It was known that there was no charge for this service.

However, at one time someone would come after we had gone to bed and put the lights out, and without our knowledge, use a mattress and sleep in the open, rejecting our help and becoming an uninvited intruder. This was not acceptable and happened for a few nights. We became aware of this because the mattress was put back differently to the way we usually stacked them. To discourage this undesirable practice, we rigged up a ten litre or two-gallon bucket of water, so that when the mattress was moved, the intruder would get an unexpected wetting. We put out the lights one night and a friend and I waited. There was a clatter and we hurried out, hoping to engage our man who was in need, but he was gone.

This story went around town, and from then on, those in need asked for help instead of helping themselves unacceptably. In Jesus' day, people were the same, for He encouraged them saying, "Ask, and it will be given to you; seek and you will find; knock, and it will be opened to you." Matthew 7:7.

Reflection: Oh Lord, thank you for the knowledge that you know what we need better than we do ourselves and before we even know.

Floods

We had a Sunday School of one hundred pupils and many of the outback children had never seen the sea. When the leaders of a holiday camp at Magnetic Island offered us the opportunity of joining them, I took thirteen young people from Mt Isa. What a time they had; sea, sand, rain, and many new friends!

After a fortnight, it was time to return home. The wet season had begun and the passenger train could go no further than Julia Creek. There was water as far as the eye could see. In the flat country, the water does not run, as it does here, in Gympie, when the Mary River floods. It seems to just walk across the country. This meant we were in for a long stay.

After two nights the train returned to Townsville. The passengers and our group were put into old box carriages for shelter. I don't remember being hungry, as the bush hospitality must have supplied food for us. However, I do remember that hygiene was rough. Toilets for the males were sheets of galvanised roofing iron, standing on their ends in a circle. Ladies used the station toilets. With no sanitary service, after days in the heat and humidity, the odour was very high. The only disinfectant available was kerosene and diesel, which was sprayed around by some men.

As the water walked away, the highest objects started to appear, the first thing being the railway line. After two more nights camped in the old box carriages, the passenger train returned and moved us on with great care. We were pleased to be going home after being marooned. There are some good Biblical principles that help at all times. Proverbs 6:22 says: "When you roam, they will lead you; when you sleep, they will keep you; and when you awake, they will speak with you."

The Bible says in Psalm 107:35; "God turns a wilderness into pools of water, and dry land into water-springs" and in verse 33 "He turns rivers into a wilderness, and the water-springs into dry ground."

Reflection: We thank you that, in your own time, you will turn the parched ground into green pastures with showers of water and water our dry lives with showers of blessings.

Upgraded

God's lessons for life are for all. One June, we had Wayne and Simone Chapman as our guest speakers, who have had their lives changed and guided by the Power of Jesus Christ. They are grain growers, cattle producers and business people living in the Taroom district. Simone was a Gympie girl. This is part of her story.

The Christian witness at The World Expo 88 was "The Pavilion of Promise." One of the Bible promises is, "In all your ways acknowledge Him and He shall direct your paths."

When Simone, daughter of Rodney and Barbara Neale, who had spent her early years on a dairy farm at Mooloo, went to the Pavilion of Promise as a hostess, she never foresaw how her life would change. She was a Bachelor of Applied Science student and had always known about God, but now became personally aware that God was in all things. Being at the Pavilion with other people who enjoyed God's love, forgiveness, and presence was a great experience for Simone.

One young man from Taroom, Wayne Chapman, a Bachelor of Rural Science, who acknowledged God in his life, also wanted Simone to be part of his future. Simone, enjoying God's love and Wayne's love, said 'Yes', and they were married in Gympie in 1989 and set up their home on a 4,300-acre property at Taroom. The dairy farm life at Mooloo had prepared her for mustering, branding cattle, planting and harvesting which was now done on a much larger scale.

God helps us with changes in circumstances. The Chapmans needed to spend five years at Emerald, where Wayne's degrees gave him employment with the D.P.I. During that time Simone experienced the pain which only a mother knows because of a miscarriage. In all happenings, God comes personally with strength and comfort and also through the love of Christian friends.

It was seven years before they could welcome into their family a baby called Joshua. The need now was for God's wisdom, in example and teaching of strong Christian truths, to give their boy purpose and power for everyday life.

The Bible says in Proverbs 22:6; "Train up a child in the way he should go, and when he is old, he will not depart from it."

Reflection: We thank you, Father, for the wisdom that only you can give.

Returned Thanks

Over the years, I have tried to make it a practice to meet new people in different walks of life. In the past, the best place was the pub, especially in small towns.

I have met manual workers who had great physical achievements; salesmen who were leaders in their realms as well as those who were responsible for satellite observation, even the lonely men who sat alone and it would take many contacts to learn why they were. I have also met the heavy machinery worker with a sense of achievement because he was able to control powerful equipment and the inventor who was working on new creations which would bring him a change in his fortunes. For others, a set of circumstances had overtaken them and they just needed a bed or a feed. They were the easy ones to help and generally we never saw or heard from them again.

Then one day, in connection with my Church, I visited a small town in central New South Wales with only one pub. I needed to call at the pub, and as I walked in, one man at the bar turned and his face lit up. He said, "I owe you five pounds ($10). Years ago, you gave me a feed in Mt. Isa." We had had an arrangement with a cafe where, for a ticket, they received sausages and plenty of potatoes enough to fill a hungry person. This man, who had been one of those recipients, had not forgotten, and years later was happy to pay while we talked about old times. God supplies all our needs and we need to take time to thank Him.

The Bible says in 1 Thessalonians 5:18: "In everything give thanks; for this is the will of God in Christ Jesus for you."

Reflection: Father, we thank You that You will supply all our needs.

Flooded

In Australia, we experience droughts and floods. In the flat country where the water walks across the land it takes days to recede. In Gympie, because of the steep slopes, there is a strong current and the water moves more quickly.

Years ago, a colleague of mine in a central New South Wales town about twenty-five miles from where we lived, rang me one morning asking for my assistance. The flood waters were moving through his town. He said, "Come by the back road and leave your car on higher ground. I will pick you up from there."

He had secured a fair sized dinghy with an outboard motor. This was prior to the SES and other official organisations being formed. We made some helpful calls and then someone remembered an elderly couple some kilometres west of the town, where the husband was ill.

We set off and it was an odd feeling to be boating down the middle of the main road out of town. On reaching the property, we found enough exposed fence to be able to tie up the boat. The water was all through the house. The wife was very distressed, not knowing what to do. Her husband was on a bed with the dog and the water was within inches of the mattress. We took the wife to the boat, settled her in and returned for the husband. As he could not walk, we cradled him between us, carrying him down the path to the front gate. In our struggle to get through the narrow gate, we dislodged a board from the ground between the gate posts. Up came the timber and a half-drowned snake. He was disturbed and thrashing about. My mate was through the gate and we could not drop our patient, so it was a matter of standing still, and much to my relief, the reptile slowly floated away.

With the couple and their dog safely in the boat, it was a slower journey back across a sports oval to a pick-up point, where the relieved couple was put into the care of concerned friends. These people, who were giving care, were finding out the truth of the words of Jesus as quoted by Paul in Acts 20:35. "It is more blessed to give than to receive."

Reflection: Thank you to those that give and please give us a spirit of giving.

The Last Swagman

Once, while living out in the west, my work required travelling many kilometres by road to the east to pick up goods from a depot. This trip involved travelling gravel roads through heavily timbered areas, good grazing land, productive grain growing country through which a good bitumen road took me to hill country, and a major town. This I was able to do in hours, which would have meant days under the old mode of travel. I would stop to help those on the road who were stranded or give a lift to someone walking.

One day, at the end of a long straight stretch of road, I could see a 'man from the past' a real 'swaggie' with his 'matilda' on his back and his 'billy' in his hand, bowyangs, which meant his trouser legs were tied just below the knees, which saved his trousers wearing out at the knees and his hat corks hanging on strings around the rim to hunt the flies away. He was making steady progress.

The clouds indicated that it was likely to rain at any time and the rain would last for several days. I pulled up, offered him a ride, and felt honoured when he accepted. As we travelled, he explained that he had been on the road for years, with a circuit which took about three years to cover, and he also knew the best spots for shelter.

Before we got too close to population, he said, "Stop when we get to the next hall". There were a number of halls, still standing, a reminder that there was once a village there which serviced Cobb & Co coaches and horse teams.

As the next hall came into view, he said, "There it is, I know how to get in and it has an open fire place. It's going to rain and I'll by dry, warm and comfortable until it's over."

That was the last swaggie I've seen on the roads and the last time I travelled that road the hall was gone. Old timers and old buildings pass away. I wonder whether our desire to give a helping hand is also passing away.

We know that our emotional and spiritual help is always available when we need help in the deep things of life for the Bible says in Hebrews 4:16 says, "Let us come boldly to the throne of grace, that we may obtain mercy and find grace to help in time of need."

Reflection: I thank you, God, that you will always provide us with shelter in the storms of life.

Christmas Prayers

In my time of study and training for the ministry, I remember one of the staff relating an experience of his grandfather, an evangelical preacher. He had preached a sermon with great freedom and made an altar call, (This just meant asking people to accept Jesus as their friend and to forgive them of their sins). Immediately a man, obviously much moved, came forward for prayer.

The preacher asked him, "What was it in my sermon that moved you?"
He replied, "Oh, I don't remember a word you said." As you can imagine this deflated the preacher but the man continued, "It was the lady with the new baby sitting in front of me. It was the wonder of new life and God's gift that made me want to seek Him in prayer."

At the first Christmas, the Baby in the manger had many different people come to worship Him . Shepherds; these were rural workers, (Luke 2) Simeon and Anna (who were prophets), ordinary people, men and women, and wise men; the learned. Read their story in Matthew 2.

In a small country town, there was an elderly man in our Church, who had no schooling, could not read, or write, and used a particular 'X' for his signature. However, he always had a job because of his work ethic and honesty. To him, the Baby in the manger, Jesus Christ, was the centre of his life. He would say, "I am going to 'evan' as he always dropped his "H"s.

On another occasion, I worked with a man completing his Agricultural Science degree. He said, "When I first went to Uni, I didn't believe in the Baby in the manger, God's Son, stuff. But as I studied the wonders of life and death, and the growth in my field of research, I realized that the Baby in the manger was God's Son for real and I became a believer". He's gone on to make a great contribution in his profession.

On yet another occasion, I sat in the office of a man whose business had grown beyond all his hopes; hardware, furniture, fertilizer, seeds, fuels, and transport. He was discussing some of his responsibilities. Before I left, I asked him if I could pray with him for guidance. He agreed, and when I finished, he was very moved. He said that he had been a worshipper most of his life. I pray for guidance to Jesus Christ, the Baby which was born in a manger, but never before has a minister bothered to pray with me here in the office.

This Christmas, whether or not you can read and write, you can believe. If you are highly educated, when you believe, you put an extra dimension to your personality. We all have decisions to make, at home or business. Prayer is the power for guidance and when it is experienced, it brings confidence.

Reflection: We thank you for the guidance that you give us day by day.

Those Good Old Days

With all the modern methods now for killing and deterring insects (flies, mosquitoes, and other creepy crawlies), gauzed homes and automatically closing doors, one easily forgets the efforts we had to make to live and sleep in peace fifty years or so ago.

Our first Church was in the North West of Queensland and mosquitoes were our number one pest. The evening church service would commence after someone had gone around the seats with a hand pump spray (atomizer). A half hour later, there would be a pause, and someone would do it all again, enabling the worshippers to continue the Service in peace, without being bitten constantly by mosquitoes.

Monday mornings we would sweep up dust pans full of mossies and dispose of them.

Sleeping was another operation requiring some skill. We slipped in under the mosquito net then pulled the hand spray in to kill the mossies which came in with us. During the night more would somehow get in.

We used to say "The big ones pushed the smaller ones through the net" and when they had feasted on us, they were too big to get out.

Our first child was born there, and as she grew and could move more easily, one night she pulled the net part way across her head. The mossies had a wonderful feed, leaving so many bites that her head was looking like she had a bad heat rash. It took days to clear the marks away.

Families needed to be resourceful in many ways, giving each other support. Their love for each other was of lasting value and has special memories which gives rise to the saying 'The good old days' instead of 'Those trying times'. I believe it was the resourcefulness and comradeship of those isolated communities, which has made these areas of Australia special.

They practiced Jesus' teaching of the Good Samaritan as in Luke 10, where an injured man was left on the roadside. A Samaritan (a person that the Jews looked down upon) went to him, bound up his wounds, set him on his beast, brought him to an inn and took care of him. When he left, he paid for his care and went guarantor for any excess expenses.

Reflection: For those who worked so hard to make our lives so comfortable today we thank you, oh Lord.

Preachers' Mistakes

Before TV and radio were common, formal education was the privilege of a few. When people had a spiritual experience, they were motivated to educate themselves by learning to read. They chose good books which lifted their quality of life and made them achievers.

A new preacher visited a country town and was full of his ecclesiastic training and quoted some out-standing phrases from old preachers of the past who had had books published. An old, plainly dressed man in the front pew, at the end of each quote, would say, "That's from Wilberforce, Spurgeon, D.L. Moody" or whoever was being quoted.

What the people needed to hear was God's power in the preacher's life or how God could affect the happenings in their own lives.

Another preacher opened his Service in prayer to God, only he was showing off his Theological training by using such words as: 'Infinite God', (meaning without limit) Immutability (unchangeable), Omnipresent (everywhere at all times), Omniscience (knows everything), Omnipotent (He is all-powerful). The old man in the front seat could stand it no longer and said in a loud voice, "Just call Him Father, and get on with the prayer." Prayer should take us into the presence of God with our thanks and requests.

Some Preachers are not only good people, but also have other talents, for example making music from a cross-cut saw, playing drinking glasses filled to different levels with water, wind or string instruments, accordions, and pianos. One such visiting preacher had a well-attended night service, ably assisted by other music and choir groups. At the conclusion, he went to the piano and played some professional pieces. The farmers, who had to rise early the next morning, wanted him to conclude.

The Preacher turned to the musical group and asked, "What would the musicians like me to play next?" An old farmer said, in a voice for all to hear, "Show me the way to go home". This caused a ripple of restrained laughter through the crowd, and so ended the night's gathering. When communicating the love of God, it needs to be done in the way which Jesus did, for in Mark 12:37 it says, "The common people heard Him gladly".

Reflection: Thank you, Father, that you have made your message simple enough that even a child can understand.

A Nesting Hen

Years ago, one of my Church friends inherited an isolated farm, with no electricity, only tank water, and no other conveniences. He had married a city girl who was a nurse. It is a wonder how some of these city girls adapt to farm life and accepted the inconveniences.

An Outhouse – Photo courtesy of Fiona Carthew

A new single minister (a city boy) came to the nearest town, this being his first church. To make him feel welcome, my friend and his wife invited him for dinner, but of course, the cows had to be milked first. This meant that it was getting late before the meal was ready.

The Reverend asked to go to the bathroom and they explained that the toilet was about forty yards away down the back yard. If you don't know about this kind of toilet, they were called 'the out house', or 'the thunder box' and other names which I won't print.

My friend's wife kept their toilet very clean; it being washed out weekly with the hot water from the copper in which the clothes had been boiled. The seat was made from long boards which went right across the width of the building with a suitable place to sit in the centre. On one side was a box containing butcher's paper (if you were well off) and if not, it held squares of newspaper. On the other side was another box holding sawdust or ashes, with a jam tin to scoop up the sawdust to tip into the pan. This was instead of the 'flush' which we have these days. This helped to reduce the odour and flies.

The wife explained all this to the new minister and apologized for not having more modern convenience for him. It was getting dark as he took his journey down the yard. Then from the outhouse they heard alarmed cries, "It's got me! It's got me!"

They rushed to the back door to see the alarmed Reverend standing outside the toilet, his trousers around his ankles, examining his hand. Realizing he had an audience, he hurriedly covered up his embarrassment. What had happened was that a farm chook had gone broody and was sitting in the sawdust box. When, in the dark, he had put his hand into the box, the hen, thinking she was about to be disturbed, fastened on to his hand with her beak. He thought a snake had bitten him. My friend hurried down to put his mind at rest, assuring him that it wasn't a snake, but a clucky chook protecting her nest.

This was followed by a good cup of tea and a meal. The Minister learned something about what the Bible says, that God wants to care for us as a hen cares for her brood. This now had real meaning for him. The verse is found in Luke 13:34b, where Jesus said, 'How often I wanted to gather your children together, as a hen gathers her brood under her wings, but you were not willing!'

Reflection: You care for us is so tender, Father, we thank you.

Off to Darwin

In the mid-fifties, we took our holidays and drove from Mt Isa to Darwin, on the old road. It was straight with only a narrow strip of bitumen. My wife was grateful to see a slight bend in the distance.

We stopped at the twenty-nine mile bore, which was the water supply for cattle, who walked in from about twenty miles around to drink. Here we enjoyed a cup of tea and continued on to Camooweal. Because white ants were a major problem here, some of the buildings had forty-four-gallon drums, filled with cement, as stumps.

Frewena Roadhouse 1976
Photo by Ken Hodge.
Obtained from flickr.com, used under licence cc4.0. Modified (cropped) by Wendy Wood
Licence terms are available on https://www.flickr.com/photos/40132991@N07/3813577263

After another easy day's drive, we arrived at the Frewena Roadhouse, which no longer exists, because of the new road. It consisted of a number of military huts; one for the bar, some for sleeping quarters, kitchen and dining room in another. It was rough, but clean, and wonderful when you were tired. There were only two staff there, so I asked, "Where is everybody?" They were all at the Brunette Races, which was the "Event of the Year" in the Northern Territory in those days. There was only a drover's cook to take care of any meals, and he told us we would be the only guests for the night. He waited on the tables direct from the kitchen.

I asked him, "Why aren't you at the races?" He replied, "Oh, I wouldn't go there! I would get paralytic drunk and someone would 'roll me' (which means, take all his money). So, I come here, put all my money at the bar and drink till it's all gone. This way, no one can steal it. I can stay here free by working in the kitchen and yard till my money is gone, then I go back and get a job droving."

When dinner was ready, John the cook came in still wearing his hat and with great courtesy asks, "So Madam, what would you like for dinner?" There was really no choice. That day, it was steak and onions. I said to my wife, "You will see a man-sized steak this time" and it was! We were not drovers, but we did not go hungry. Then there were sweets and by this time, John had had more of his drink and his bush style came to the fore. When he came for our order for sweets, he said, "Now Mum, what do you want, and your old man, what will he have?"

This was good country food, served in great outback style. Together with a good night's sleep and a wonderful breakfast, we were on our way westward toward the Three Ways, which was a T junction where you either turned south to Alice Springs or north to Darwin. We still had many miles of straight and narrow road to travel to Darwin.

The way to life, Jesus says in Matthew 7:14, is "Because straight is the gate, and narrow is the way, which leadeth unto life, and few there be that find it."

Reflection: For the twists and turns in our lives we thank you, oh Father, because they add growth to our personalities.

Still off to Darwin

When we arrived at the 'Three Ways', there was a 'cross' as a John Flynn Memorial and that was all! Now there is a Road House. How things change for the benefit and security of the traveling public.

We drove on to Mataranka, stopping to rest for a day at the Thermal Pools. These pools are quite small and warm, which is very different to the hot pools around Julia Creek that are fed from the hot artesian bores. In those days, the banks of the Mataranka Pools were held together by a mat of Tee Tree roots. These trees flourished because there were very few tourists to disturb them.

A few weeks earlier, film makers had used these warm springs in some scenes in the film "Jedda" and some imitation crocodiles used in the production were still in place there. During the day we were there, there was one other camper arrived. So far on our trip, we don't remember meeting or passing another vehicle on the road.

Motor vehicles were still to become popular in serving the area, as there were few easily traversed roads in the Northern Territory. The Police Force was doing away with horses in favour of motor vehicles. So, change was coming!

From here, we drove on to Katherine, where we met friends, who took us with them to Church on Sunday.

On Monday, being a holiday, our friends took us in an ex-military jeep to Katherine Gorge. At that time there were no tourist guides, so we could only go with someone who knew the way. The grass on both sides of the track was high, so even the locals could easily have taken the wrong turn. At the Gorge, the high cliffs, their colours changing with the varied rays of the sun, were awesome. Their reflection in the clear river was spectacular. All this was possible because of the power of water over the centuries. It was an amazing wonder, the grandeur of it all made us feel very small. The amount of water flowing in the Katherine River was hard for my mind to comprehend. The traces of European man were almost non-existent, except for a mob of feral donkeys, too numerous to count, whose ancestors had escaped from the early explorers.

Back in the Katherine village, the locals told us that, during World War II, the Japanese aircraft had flown as far south as Katherine, looking for the Darwin water supply, and by mistake had tried to bomb their bridge over the Katherine River. Years later we saw a documentary by the Leyland Bros. showing the Katherine Gorge in all of its splendour. How things have changed! Now TV viewers can marvel at the wonder of it all from the comfort of their own lounge rooms.

In Colossians 1:16 it says, "For by Him all things were created that are in Heaven and that are on earth, visible and invisible, whether thrones or dominions or principalities or powers, all things were created through Him and for Him."

Reflection: Lord, I thank you for the splendour of your creation.

The Effects of War

Those of us living in the Eastern and Southern States of Australia were unaware of the effect the war had in the North. All the news we received was controlled. We had some inconvenience, such as food and petrol rationing, black-outing of homes and work places. Schools had trenches dug for the children to go into in the case of air raids and this meant regular practice evacuation of the class rooms.

Fund raising was held at every opportunity, comfort parcels were made and sent to the troops; appeals were made for the giving of aluminium for the manufacture of planes. People put out pots, saucepans and anything made of aluminium in front of their houses and these were collected. Those who possessed modern vehicles had to surrender them for the military services. People living in cities and along the coast, who had relatives or friends inland, were sent to those who could take them in. That's how I met my wife.

I had seen the results of the war on Horn Island, which is near Thursday Island, and the wrecks of planes on the beach along the west coast of Cape York. However, it was still a surprise for us, as we drove into Darwin, to see the extent of the damage still evident from the seventy odd Japanese air raids.

In the flat where we stayed, there was a large bomb hole in the backyard, where the residents threw their discarded tins and bottles, and in the 1950's they were still only covering the bottom. Some people featured bomb shells in their gardens. Because of the twenty-foot high tides in the north, ship wrecks, destroyed during the raids, were visible in the harbour at low tide.

Forty-four-gallon drums, with camouflage nets drawn over them, still covered the town's water supply. The reason for this was that the authorities had needed to protect their water supply. The shell of the Post Office was all that was left standing as a tragic reminder of a direct hit in the first raid.

We have heard some of the undesirable reports about the Fanny Bay Gaol, but when we went there with a Church group to hold a Sunday service, we found each cell had a radio and fan. Some inmates were allowed to go out to work for about five hours a day. These are some of the successes which are not reported as readily as the undesirable inefficiencies.

Time had run out, and we had to hurry home. We went from Darwin to Tennant Creek. About sunset, twenty-five kilometres from Tennant Creek, we hit a big old man kangaroo. Fortunately, our car had a heavy steel bumper bar, so there was a dead kangaroo but no major damage to our car. We made it to Tennant Creek, stayed the night, then back to work the next day.

Our observations in Darwin reminded us of the Bible verse in Ecclesiastes 9:18. "Wisdom is better than weapons of war; but one sinner destroys much good."

Reflection: Lord, I thank you for your promise that one day swords will be turned into plough shears.

Leprosy

While in Darwin, my wife visited the Leprosarium. We had known about a Leprosarium in Sydney and Queensland which had been closed down and we assumed that this disease had been eradicated in Australia.

It was quite enlightening to us to find our friends were making a visit to such a facility. My wife accompanied them and took some notes which we found recently. There were buildings for residents, a modern hospital, X-Ray room plus a dark room for development. They did their own blood testing; an inmate was qualified to read the results, there was a theatre for minor operations and a labour ward.

Stress occurred because the babies had to be taken from their mothers to protect them from the disease. There were those who were advanced cases before they came in from the bush. After treatment, some were without hands, and because of damage to their feet and legs, others had stumps. There was one who was also deaf and dumb. Those who were diagnosed early, appeared to be beautifully healthy.

They had sports fields for daytime activities, and at night there were movies, table tennis and badminton. Schooling was half-a-day for maths, spelling, reading and hygiene. Drawing, sewing, and cooking were also taught.

Their huts were painted to their own personal liking and decorated with bush hunting scenes. The natives had built their own Church. It was beautifully finished with cushions on pews for comfort.

Since those days, I have read about the challenge of leprosy in the top end among indigenous tribes up until the late 1920's. Some of the missionary workers feared that, if there was not extensive help given, many would die and the loss of their culture would be very regrettable. In the years from 1986 to 2002, new leprosy cases notified to the Kimberly Public Health Unit were 28, aged from 8 years to 63. All were indigenous except one.

With care and better medicines, things have changed, workers putting into practice, the Bible verse which says, "Casting all your care upon Him, for He cares for you". 1 Peter 5:7.

Reflection: For those who work in the medical fields, Lord ,I thank you for their dedication and passion to help those in need.

Saying Grace

In the days when animal power was mainly used, men would leave the house early to feed the horses, other animals and milk the cows, before having breakfast with the family. Lunches were packed, no take-away then, and dinner at night was the time the whole family came together.

A common practice was the 'saying of grace' before the family meal, which is a short prayer thanking God for His provision. Some people called it 'asking the blessing'.

The following are a couple of examples:
1.   "We thank Thee, Lord for this good food. Bless it to us and us to Your service. Amen"
2.   "Lord, as You blessed the loaves and fishes, bless this food upon our dishes. Amen"

Nurses from the local hospital, where my aunt was training, often visited our home on their 'days off'. On one such visit, at the evening meal, my father said grace, praying the first prayer as above. One young nurse looked up before commencing her meal and said, "You really meant that prayer, didn't you?" and he always did.

With today's change in lifestyle, TV dinners, take-away, and people working long distances from home, many people do not have a family meal together very often, and miss out on this sharing experience. Our authorities wonder why there is little bonding of families these days, when one of the best family experiences is not always enjoyed together.

As Ministers, we witness different experiences, such as the following:

One of our friends was doing visitation and a lady asked him to stay for a meal. She and her son appeared to have very few earthly goods, but he felt he should accept, lest he should offend them. After they were seated, there was a pause. A Minister being present, the mother said to her son, "Tommy, you say grace". There was an even longer pause, then a flustered lad, bowed his head and said, "Round and round the table, fill your belly while you're able". The Minister then added his blessing and enjoyed their genuine hospitality.

Once on a trip to a central town in New South Wales, I was hosted by the Postmaster and his wife, who had no children. After a good night's rest, I came out for breakfast. There was an extra chair and plate at the table. Before we started the meal, they called their Fox Terrier dog, he sat on the chair and they placed his dog food on the extra plate. The Postmaster said, "Say grace, Trixie". The dog put his front paws on the table and gave a real Canine rendition of grace, with whines, howls, and barks. Then we all enjoyed breakfast.

The Scripture says in Galatians 5:18. "In everything give thanks."

Reflection: Lord, I thank you for the blessing of parents that love you and serve you faithfully.

Other Books by this Author

All these books are available as eBooks

Turning Water into Wine – 2ⁿᵈ Edition
100 Stories of God's Hand in Life

More Water into Wine – 2ⁿᵈ Edition
100 Stories of God's Hand in Life

Still More Water into Wine
100 Stories of God's Hand in Life

365 Glasses of Wine – Revised Edition
Short Devotionals for each day of the year

Conversations with Myself – Volume 1 2ⁿᵈ Edition
100 Stories of Hope, Faith and Determination

Whispers from on High
Poems and short stories

Follow Helen Brown on:
Facebook: https://www.facebook.com/HelenBrownCollection/

Instagram: https://www.instagram.com/helen_brown_books/

Pinterest: https://www.pinterest.com.au/helenbrown58726/

www.ingramcontent.com/pod-product-compliance
Lightning Source LLC
Chambersburg PA
CBHW050309010526
44107CB00055B/2169